The
ART
of
ACTING

From Basic Exercises to
Multidimensional Performances

by
CARLTON COLYER

Foreword by
ARTHUR STORCH

MERIWETHER PUBLISHING LTD.
Colorado Springs, Colorado

Meriwether Publishing Ltd., Publisher
P.O. Box 7710
Colorado Springs, CO 80933

Editor: Arthur Zapel
Typesetting: Sharon Garlock
Cover illustration (oil painting): Arthur Zapel
Book design: Michelle Z. Gallardo

© Copyright MCMLXXXIX Meriwether Publishing Ltd.
Printed in the United States of America
First Edition

Library of Congress Cataloging-in-Publication Data

Colyer, Carlton.
    The art of acting : from basic exercises to multidimensional
performances / by Carlton Colyer : foreword by Arthur Storch.
       p.   cm.
    Includes bibliographical references.
    ISBN 0-916260-62-3
    1. Acting. I. Title.
PN2061.C64   1989
792'.028--dc20   89-27928
                                                  CIP

I dedicate this book to my immediate family on whose love I depend, especially my mother, Charlotte, who is more responsible for my writing this book than she realizes, and my son, Cameron, who was with me as this book was being written.

TABLE OF CONTENTS

FOREWORD

Carlton Colyer has a depth of experience in theatre that few other people have. He was a working actor for twenty years, playing well over two hundred parts in theatre, television and movies. He has played opposite some of the theatre's most talented leading actresses: Helen Hayes, Gloria Swanson, Tallulah Bankhead, Betty White, Betty Fields, Ruth White and Vivian Nathan. Carlton has been honored for his work by being made a lifetime member of The Actors Studio.

For the past seventeen years he has doubled as a single parent and a teacher of theatre. Carlton has been a visitng professor of theatre at Syracuse University, Brown University and the University of Rhode Island. In addition, he has headed The Syracuse in London, England, theatre program.

Carlton has directed over fifty productions ranging from Greek tragedy to contemporary comedy. He brings the best out of his actors, who always work with relaxation and confidence. They create an ensemble of dimensional characters. His interpretation of plays is simple, clear and true to the playwright's purpose.

Today, Carlton is teaching acting, voice production and theatre theory to adults and gifted teenagers, but he also spends time bringing the discipline and fun of acting to the very young, the underprivileged, the mentally retarded and the emotionally disturbed. He believes a working knowledge of theatre belongs to everyone.

Carlton teaches theatre because he wants to teach. It is as a teacher that he is doing his best theatre work. And now he has decided to put what he knows into a book about acting technique. His book presents the best work of the best actors, teachers and directors with whom he has been associated.

The Art of Acting includes almost everything one needs to know about creating believable, multidimensional human characters. There is something for everybody in this book. It includes exercises to develop technique, instructions for creating a character and building a role, and discussions of period style, theatrical modes and dramatic forms. It teaches actors to depend on themselves when creating characters and building roles. There is nothing in this book that is not useful.

This book is full of clearly stated information, but it also includes anecdotes and opinions to back up that information.

It can be used by individuals as a step-by-step training guide. It can also be used as a reference for terms, exercises and concepts. It is not a book to read and put aside but to put to use again and again.

I congratulate Carlton on the work he has done, and I encourage the reader to get started and put this book to work.

Arthur Storch
Broadway Director;
Chairman, Syracuse University
Drama Department

ACKNOWLEDGEMENTS

Alan Alda, Susan Arundale, Edward Asner, Jennifer Aubin, The Balakians, Michael and Cornelia Bessie, Shelly Bleeker, The Brown Learning Community, Candy and Gertrude Cane, Ethel Cates, John Emigh, The Franklins, Wrenn Goodrum, Ronnie Jenkins, Zachery Morowitz, Clare Orme, Bill Osborne, The Rhode Island State Council on the Arts, The Seagliones, Jonathan Schwartz, Joyce Stevos, Arthur Storch, Michael Thomas, Rose Wanner, Max Winter, Arthur Zapel.

Bob Barsamian, Ellen Blickman, Sherry Bloom, Robert Bonoto, Kristin Brady, Kristine Brown, Margaret Brockie, Sue Buffington, Henry Butler, Ronald Cauette, Ellen Colyer, The Stephen Colyers, Chase Crosby, Sloan and Judith Danenhower, Eric Dellums, Susan Devine, Lisa Diaz, Margaret Doner, Sandy Dornick, Malcom Duffy, Michael Eagan, Laura Ellsworth, Leif Ericson, Vanessa Gilbert, Karen Greco, Edward Greer, Helen Hayes, Jamie Hendry, Francis Hidden, Fred Hutchinson, Ray Hynes, Sara Jones, Jerry Kahn, Elia Kazan, Jim Kelly, Dale Lawrence, Gail Lepkowski, Jonathan Lester, E. Floyd Loonsbury, Randy Lutterman, Jamie Meyer, Linda (Rough) Nave, Bill and Susan Needle, Ashley Olmstead, Fifi Oscard, Ben Piazza, Daisy Prince, Michael Roberts, Betty Rollin, Michael Rubin, Pat Sales, Chuck Schuster, Bob Selnick, Cyril Simon, Bruce Smith, The Spurwink School II, Lee Strasberg, Gloria Swanson, Julie Warner, Les and Sue Wells, Ruth White and Don Wilmeth.

INTRODUCTION

This book will present the most useful facts I know about the art of acting. It presents acting as a process, the elements of which should be of value to everybody, both the beginning acting student and the experienced actor.

I teach acting today with prejudices established after twenty years of professional acting and another twenty years of teaching acting. I was taught to act by a protégé of David Belasko, the father of naturalistic theatre in the United States, and by various teachers, including Lee Strasberg of the Stanislavski Technique. Midway through my acting career I was honored by being made a lifetime member of the Actors Studio. Because of my training and the good experience I had putting that training to work, I am what might be labeled a Method actor and a teacher of the Method. I prefer to think of myself, however, as a proponent of a technique of acting that focuses on the creation, on stage or in front of a camera, of multidimensional, human characters.

I believe in individual interpretation but I also believe the individual should have some basic precepts on which to base his or her interpretation. This book presents the best techniques of the best actors and teachers I have known. It will not present exercises for exercise's sake, but exercises to help you become a proficient actor.

I am not a teacher of acting who would prefer to be an actor, a director or a playwright. I am an experienced actor and director who became more interested in the process of actors' work than in the results of that work. I teach people who are ambitious to become professional actors. I also teach gifted teen-agers, vocational-technical students, emotionally disturbed children, disadvantaged children and mentally retarded people. I think the art of acting should be available to everybody.

This book is written, however, for people who want to go beyond just dabbling in the art of acting. When I teach potential professionals, I try to teach them to be artist-actors, not just performing professionals. I take great joy in my work and the work of my students. This book is designed to share that joy with you. Beware, however: the only way I know toward the source of that joy is through serious hard work.

This book will begin with what I believe should be the beginning of the artist-actor's training process. Many actors' training courses only give lip service to fundamentals. Because, however, I believe in a complete process, I have been as thorough with the basic precepts as I have been in seeing them through to their logical conclusions.

Focused energy, relaxation and concentration are the characteristics of the work of a good actor. Like good athletes, good actors have the ability to channel their nervous energy. They can relax and think on their feet and put their thoughts to work. Good actors are relaxed in their work even though the characters they are portraying may be under a nervous strain. You are never conscious that they are trying hard to perform. This book will teach you to focus your energy, relax and concentrate on your actors' work.

Good acting has as its goal the recreation of multidimensional, human behavior because human behavior is much more fascinating and exciting than is fake theatrical behavior. Learning to be a fine actor is not learning to behave theatrically but learning to behave as a human being while in a theatrical situation. This book will present the best methods I know for your becoming a fine actor.

Carlton Colyer

I. BUILDING A TECHNIQUE

ENSEMBLE ACTING: Each individual character should relate to the other characters as multidimensional human beings where there is no star actor who must be in the spotlight. (Cast of <u>The Time Trial</u>, by Jack Gilhooley, a Syracuse University Drama Department production.)

1. An Introduction to Useful Acting Terms

This book is designed to serve both beginning and experienced actors. Beginners may consider themselves lucky for they don't have bad habits to unlearn. Experienced actors should consider this book an opportunity to reinforce, add to, and even correct the technique they already have.

So that we have a vocabulary in common, let me introduce to you some of the useful terms used by actors and directors:

STUDIO: *A classroom or a rehearsal space — sometimes a big empty space and sometimes a room cluttered with folding chairs and seedy, early Salvation Army furniture. Soon, you will learn to change this empty space or this clutter into a fascinating world of your own creation.*

OFFSTAGE or OFF CAMERA: *Where, if you can't see the audience or the camera lens, they or it can't see you. More importantly, the area where an actor prepares to enter the onstage or on camera area. A good actor never comes into the acting area from offstage; he comes from where his character was. For instance, if the character supposedly has just climbed many flights of stairs, the actor comes on stage out of breath. If the character has just had an exciting experience, the actor comes on stage emotionally excited.*

ONSTAGE or ON CAMERA: *Where the actor behaves and expresses himself while in character. The place where the actor makes his character available to the audience or the camera — the place where the actor brings his character to life.*

CAMERA RIGHT and LEFT: *Right and left of the camera's lens from behind the camera. The actor's right and left, as he faces the camera, is the opposite of camera right and left.*

STAGE RIGHT and LEFT: *The actor's right and left*

as he faces the audience.

DOWNSTAGE: *The area of the stage toward the audience.*

UPSTAGE: *The area of the stage away from the audience.*

UPSTAGING: *Taking the audience's attention away from another actor. If you maintain an upstage position in relation to the other actors on the stage, you force an actor who wants to face you to turn his back on the audience. An actor, however, can upstage you without being upstage of you. I worked with a star actress who, during my big scene with her, would sit downstage on the downstage edge of a desk. Whenever she felt that I was getting more than my fair share of the audience's attention, she would shake her famous long blonde tresses until they fell in her face. When she knew she had the audience's attention, she would put her hair back into place with a flip of her head. I learned to wait, in character of course, until her act was over. Then I would go on with the play.*

BLOCKING: *Directions given by a director about where an actor should move in the acting area. Blocking on a stage is usually given with a direction to move downstage, upstage, stage right and left or center stage. The actor can also be asked to move in relation to furniture or to another actor. Camera directors often use stage directions when giving blocking but you may be asked by a camera director to hit marks — to move to and then stand on an exact spot marked by tape on the floor.*

CHEATING or PLAYING THREE-QUARTERS: *This refers to being fair to a fellow actor and at the same time to the audience. If a scene has been staged on a proscenium stage with two actors facing each other, the audience only sees a profile of each actor. If both actors turn three-quarters toward the audience, they can share the audience's attention and still relate to each other.*

A PROSCENIUM THEATRE: *A theatre in which the stage is separated from the audience by a proscenium arch. The audience witnesses the action of the play through this arch. If it were the real world, it would be obvious that everything in a ninety-degree arc of the acting area is missing. In the theatre world, this space is often treated by the actors as if it were actually a wall or other obstruction making them unaware of the audience. For this reason the proscenium arch is sometimes referred to as the fourth wall. Actors are said to break the fourth wall when they relate directly to the audience.*

A STAGE WITH AN APRON: *A stage that extends beyond the proscenium arch into the audience. From Renaissance times until the middle of the nineteenth century most indoor theatres had stages with large aprons where most of the dramatic action took place. The area behind the proscenium arch contained the scenery and was more of a background to the action than it was an acting space. It was after the middle of the nineteenth century that the acting space was separated from the audience and moved behind the proscenium arch.*

ENVIRONMENTAL THEATRE: *A relatively recent attempt to do away with the convention of separating the audience from the performers with an imaginary fourth wall. In traditional proscenium theatres, the stage, or the apron of the stage, if there is one, is often extended well out into the audience becoming what is called a thrust stage. The auditorium and its aisles are sometimes used as acting space. This makes for a more intimate, immediate relationship between the audience and the actors. In environmental theatre there usually isn't a traditional setting to create the illusion of the place where the dramatic action is happening. The people in the audience have to use their imaginations and share with the actors and sound and lights people, the responsibility of making the make-believe place believable.*

People are beginning to realize with the advent of environmental theatre, that theatre can take place anywhere as long as the dramatic action is available to the audience. Theatre is no longer limited to theatres. Most theatre schools and some professional theatre complexes now have a production space that is just that, a large empty space or room, usually painted black — a black box. In such a space you can create any relationship between the audience and the actors that you want to create.

Shakespeare's Globe Theatre was known in its time as a public theatre but, by today's standards, it might have been called an environmental theatre.

THEATRE-IN-THE-ROUND: *Theatre with the audience placed 360 degrees around the acting area. Actors and directors have to see to it that the actors frequently turn and face in different directions so that each section of the audience gets a fair share of seeing each actor's face.*

CREATING A CHARACTER: *Using yourself and your experience and research to create a dimensional human being who will come to life on stage or in front of a camera. Creating a character is not putting on a costume and make-up and magically turning into someone else.*

BUILDING A ROLE: *Creating a character within the context of a screenwriter's or a playwright's script. In mainstream theatre a role is built during a rehearsal period with a director in charge of interpreting the playwright's script. It is the actor's task to create his own character with research, homework and rehearsal .and to adapt that character to fill the role given the character by the director.*

IN CHARACTER: *The ideal state for an actor to be in while rehearsing and performing: the stage in which the actor thinks, feels and behaves as his character would think, feel and behave. Being in character is not thinking such thoughts as "What's my next line?," "I hope the audience and the director love me," or "I hope I get good reviews and become rich and famous."*

Once you have learned to build a character and to stay in character, you will have learned most of what there is to learn about good acting.

REPRESENTATIONAL ACTING: *Being the character you have created: behaving, feeling and thinking in character. In other words, good acting.*

DEMONSTRATIONAL ACTING: *Not staying in character when you are supposed to be in character: standing outside your character and showing the audience or indicating to the audience what your character is supposedly thinking and feeling. Using phony or mechanical physical or vocal expression to demonstrate how your character is thinking or feeling. In other words, bad acting.*

OVERACTING: *An exaggerated form of demonstrational acting. Being over theatrical or hammy: mugging or making distorted faces at the audience; making out of character remarks to the audience. Trying to manipulate the audience.*

Shakespeare fired his famous comedian, Will Kempe, for overacting.

ENSEMBLE ACTING: *Acting in a company of actors that believes each individual character should relate to the other characters as multidimensional human beings, where there is no star actor who must be in the spotlight and constantly having the audience's attention focused on him.*

ANTICIPATING: *Instead of having a human experience and reacting to it naturally, reacting to a dramatic experience before you or your character has a chance to have that experience. Deciding beforehand what your character's reaction to an experience should be.*

It may surprise you that a teacher of multidimensional acting would begin by introducing you to technical terms about the mechanics of the acting space and the relationship of the actor to the audience or camera. I believe what we fear the most is the unknown. If you have a sense of where the actor works and in general what sort of work is expected from a good actor, you may feel more comfortable about going to work. Of course, the more tools and technique you develop, the more comfortable you will be. So let's get to work to learn command of both the tools and the technique.

Physical exercises locate and warm up the limbs, muscles and joints, energize and relax the body, and initiate an actor's creative physical expression. (Acting class, Providence, Rhode Island.)

2. WARMING UP EXERCISES

THE LIMBS, MUSCLES AND THE JOINTS

Your actor's instrument is yourself and the total instrument needs to be tuned before it can do an actor's work. Physical expression is just as important, if not more important, in acting as is vocal expression. I have a set of physical exercises that are multipurpose and fun to do. The exercises locate and warm up the limbs, muscles and joints, energize and relax the body, and initiate an actor's creative physical expression.

Each of my students works in a space in which he can comfortably stretch out one leg and both arms in any direction and not interfere with another student.

Freeing the Ankles, Neck and Shoulders

We begin the first exercise by standing in place with both feet flat on the floor. Then, keeping our upper bodies straight, we move our bodies in circles using only our ankles for the rotation. Next, we raise our arms and become trees swaying in the breeze with our roots in the ground but our ankles free to allow us to sway and rotate.

There are seven spinal vertebrae between the Atlas bone inside the middle of the back of the skull at the top of the spine and the spine's vertebra at the base of the neck. Using only those seven vertebrae we gently move our heads in circles, side to side, and backward and forward. While we move our heads and free our necks, we let gravity have our arms so they hang at our sides. We feel our shoulders relax as our arms hang down and our heads rotate on the seven vertebrae.

Freeing the Hip Joints

Next, we imagine a smelly cigar alternately under the toe pads of each foot. We grind the cigar into the floor while poking

11

with our finger tips to locate where the ball and socket of each hip joint is working. Having located and freed our hip joints, we imagine a heavy barbell on the floor in front of us. We bend from the hip joints and knees and grasp the barbell with our knuckles facing forward and we lift the heavy barbell to our waists. We create an imaginary object and use dynamic tension, caused by lifting the imaginary weight, to warm up our legs, arms and stomach muscles.

Eagles

Next, we turn ourselves into eagles. Standing in place, we use our arms, wrists and fingers as wings and feathers, and then putting our knees, hip joints and ankles to work, we "fly" high into the air while standing in place. Staying within his own space, each student can then move his feet and fly or glide in circles at any dizzying height he chooses to imagine.

Swinging and Walking

We create an imaginary swing. We grasp the ropes or chains, sit into the imaginary seat and, crouching in place, we pull on the pretend ropes and rock back and forth on our heels and toes. As our knees and hip joints get into the act, we feel as if we were swinging way up in the air.

Next, we walk in place using our heels, toes, hip joints and knees with our arms swinging naturally. Now, we walk in circles with imaginary ten-pound weights attached to our feet. Then, we move as if we were barefoot making our way over a field filled with sharp rocks, without saying "Ouch!" until we have stepped on a make-believe rock and it hurts. Next, we pretend we are walking on the moon with very little gravity to hold us down. With each step we rise on our toes and let our arms fly in the air.

Gorillas, Samsons, Amazons and Spaghetti

We bend forward slightly from the knees and hips, let our arms hang heavy and turn ourselves into gorillas. We pretend we are standing in the portico of a Greek temple with stone pillars at arms' length on either side of us and a stone ceiling at arms' length above our heads. An earthquake begins to shake the temple but we pretend we are Samson or a giant Amazon woman and we can hold up and push back the pillars and hold up the ceiling when it comes crashing down on us. We give the pillars and ceiling enough weight so we have to work hard to push them back into place. In other words, we create obstacles to getting the work done. Once again dynamic tension has been warming up our limbs and muscles.

To loosen up and to relax our tense muscles, we pretend we are a bunch of spaghetti standing in a pot of water. The water begins to boil and we gradually go limp and, suspended in the boiling water, we begin to bubble and shake — first our fingers, then thumbs, wrists, elbows, whole arms, head on the seven vertebrae, ankles, knees and hip joints. We loosen up our muscles and every joint of every limb of our bodies.

Let It All Go

Finally, we create imaginary guitars and drum sets and set up a rhythm with them. Then we put away the make-believe instruments and dance and move to our own rhythm anywhere and any way we want to without bumping into each other.

After we have done this series of exercises a couple of times, we have a routine any one of us could lead. We put on some rock and roll or jazz, anything with a strong beat. One of us gets up on a table or a platform and leads us to the music from one exercise to the next. We have our own warm-up routine.

Make up your own series of exercises. Be creative but put all the limbs and joints to work and alternate tension with loosening exercises.

Childhood Spirit

This set of exercises may seem kind of childlike but that's part of the purpose of it. It has been said that learning to act is allowing yourself to return to that childhood spirit you had when you had the energy and the lack of self-consciousness to involve yourself in such games as Space Men or Space Women, Cowboys and Indians or "I'm Daddy, You're Mommy and He's Baby." My seventeen-year-old son preserves that spirit when he grabs a Nerf ball and acts out a whole basketball game with him as the hero who finally saves the game with a second to play. Let yourself go! Regain some of that spontaneous spirit. Childhood energy and a sense of pretending is essential to good acting.

Comments and Advice

The warm-up exercises I do with student actors are not designed to condition your body. If you want to thoroughly condition your body — and you should want to do this — there are experts with whom you should study. Take Tai Chi, Karate or fencing lessons. Study with a stage combat expert or a teacher of mime. Take a course or read a book about good dietary habits. Take dancing lessons: ballet, modern or tap. You can find work in today's musical theatre only if you are a "triple threat": a dancer-singer-actor. If you have athletic prowess, continue to be active in sports. You will keep your body limber and trim and many of the disciplines of athletics are complementary to the discipline of acting. Athletes have made some of the best actors I have known. Above all, never lose sight of the fact that physical expression is a very important aspect of an actor's creative work.

THE FACE

Facial Expression

Good actors don't make faces on stage or in front of a camera; they allow facial expressions to evolve out of the experiences their characters are having. Before, however, the face is alive enough to express itself freely, it may need some stretching and warming up. I get my students to make faces, not to teach them how to manufacture phony facial expressions, but to get their facial muscles loosened up so their facial expressions will happen organically and spontaneously.

Clown Faces

My students make clown faces. Without make-up they make grotesque mask-like faces. They distort their faces, stretching their jaws, tongues, eyebrows and foreheads. They even try to get their noses and ears into the act.

We do it quickly. I'll say, "Relax. Close your eyes. Happy clown. One-Two-Go. Extend. Freeze it. Relax." And so on. On "Go," they make their faces express the idea I have suggested. On "Extend," they stretch their facial expressions as far as they will go. I freeze their faces until I am sure each student can feel the expression he or she has created. You can make up a whole list of clown faces: happy, sad, angry, shy, stupid, ugly, pretty, etc., and go to it. Get a partner. Encourage each other to be ridiculous and grotesque. Don't copy each other; make your own huge, fun facial expressions. Make clown faces by yourself in front of a mirror. Bring your face alive to make the expression you ask it to make. Work spontaneously. Don't think about what your face should look like; just name the facial expression and make it quickly.

Organic Expression

Now it's time to stop manufacturing expressions; let your face express itself. Look in a mirror. Relax. Think of the person you love the most or dislike the most. Think of his eyes or hair. Listen to his voice. Pick specific aspects of the person to think about. Don't make faces. Let your face react to what you are remembering. See, your face reflects your love or dislike without your telling it to. Sure, your facial expressions are more subtle than the clown faces you made, and they should be. They are honest, human reactions to what you are thinking and feeling.

If you don't think your face is alive enough yet, do another set of clown faces. You will soon have such a mobile face that you can trust it to express itself by itself. You will have to make a concerted effort for it not to reveal what you are thinking or feeling.

THE VOICE

Of all the aspects of the actor's instrument the voice may be the most difficult to tune and to keep in tune. For the vocal mechanism to work properly, it often must be freed from bad habits and allowed to work as nature originally intended it to work. Before you can free your natural voice, you should know how it works.

Breathing

As simply as I can put it, the vocal instrument is a system dependent on full breathing, resonation, articulation, amplification and projection. Breath is the energy on which the whole system rides. The breath you take in to create vocal sound should fill your lungs. It is allowed to do this when your diaphragm muscle, a thin flat muscle attached to the bottom of your rib cage, tips so that your rib cage floats up and away from your lungs, allowing them to fill with air.

The Bellows

Instead of asking my students to breathe into their lungs or their diaphragms, I ask them to imagine a bellows built into them. A bellows is that object used to make glowing coals in a fireplace blaze up to relight the fire. It has arms, an accordian-like body and a nozzle. Imagine that the nozzle of your bellows is your mouth. The arms of your bellows are the latisimus muscles along the sides of the trunk of your body. The squeeze box of your bellows is your stomach. To take a full breath, you think the arms of your bellows open. As you think the arms away from the sides of your body, open your mouth and feel the cool air flow in over your hard palate. Don't breathe through your nose. Feel your stomach expand.

Natural Breathing

This may not be what happens to you normally when you take a full breath, but it should be. This is how nature intended us to take a full breath. You can prove this to yourself by being conscious of how you breathe after you have run hard or after you have climbed a few flights of stairs. Even better, test your breathing when you are in bed and just about to fall asleep. Roll over on your back. Put your hands on your tummy and feel what happens. More than likely you are breathing through your mouth. Your breaths are gentle but deep. As the air flows into you, your tummy expands. As it flows out, your tummy contracts. No matter what bad habits society and your psyche have taught you, that is how your breathing mechanism should work every time you take a full breath that will support good vocal sound.

If you are sitting down reading this and you can't get your breathing mechanism to work as I have described, get up. Stand up and bend forward over your hip joints. Double over until your head is pointing at the floor. Let your arms hang down toward the floor. Now use your imaginary bellows to take a deep breath. Think the arms open and feel the cool air flow in your mouth. Feel your stomach expand. Don't use your stomach as a muscle to breathe with. Free it to expand and contract of its own accord. It may take some time but you should be able to get your breathing mechanism to work as well while you are standing or sitting as it does when you are tipped upside-down or you are lying relaxed on your back.

Advice About Breathing

You may have subconsciously trained your stomach to help hold up the trunk of your body when you are sitting or standing and it doesn't want to free itself to become the accordian of your bellows. It wants to contract when it should be expanding and you can't make it behave itself. If you continue to have major problems taking a natural, full breath, don't try to train your voice by yourself. Take voice lessons or singing lessons. You can't free your natural voice unless you can free your breathing mechanism to work as nature intended it to work.

If you can use your bellows to take a full breath, then make using it a habit. Breathe fully when you speak in everyday life. Breathe fully when you do physical exercises. Breathe fully while you are doing vocal warm-ups. Don't hesitate to use your bellows when you need breath to support vocal sound. Don't wait to breathe until you end a thought. If you need a breath to make the next sound, breathe.

Vowel and Consonant Sounds

The breath you take in to support vocal expression is a stream of airwaves, vibrant with your thoughts and feelings. When you take a full breath, that breath forms a pool of vibrations in the center of you. As you voice your thoughts and feelings that pool of vibrations sends a stream of vibrations up your windpipe, or larynx. The vocal chords sometimes add more vibrations to the stream. These vibrations become the vowel sounds of speech. The only pure vowel sound the vocal chords can make is "Aaah." The articulators mold that "Aaah" sound to form the rest of the vowel sounds.

Articulators

Your articulators are your jaw, cheeks, teeth, lips and tongue. They work together not only to mold the vowel sounds but also to make the consonant sounds. Make some vowel and consonant sounds and see if I'm not right. As we go along we will free the articulators to do their work.

Resonation

The most vibrant sounds, the vowel sounds, want a place to resound. Vowel sounds will flow naturally to the resonators if you let them flow there. Your most important resonators are your chest cavity, your mouth and its hard palate — the front of the roof of your mouth — your sinus cavities and your nose. Your sinus cavities and nose are called the mask resonator. Your chest cavity is your woofer where the low tones want to resonate. Your mask is your tweeter where the higher tones want to resonate. Your mouth is where sound is made into resonant language.

The places where vibrant sound usually gets stuck and is never properly resonated are your throat and the soft palate or adenoid area. That's why you may have a throaty voice or what's known as a nasal voice. By the way — the nose is a perfectly good resonator. It is sound that gets stuck in the spongy area behind your nose that makes your voice sound as if you had a cold.

Advice About Vocal Chords

If you want a resonant voice with tonal variety and you should, you have to learn to free those vibrant vowel sounds. First of all, disassociate your vocal chords from anything but their initiation of that pure "Aaah" sound. That's all your vocal chords should do, initiate that sound. They don't make consonant sounds. They weren't

17

made to project your voice. When you use your vocal chords to amplify vocal sound, you end up screaming and screeching. You end up hoarse. If you keep it up long enough, you'll grow nodes on your chords that may have to be surgically removed.

Opening the Throat

To free sound to travel out of your throat and into the resonators, you must learn to keep your throat open. You can open your throat by training the muscles in the root of your tongue to relax. Put the tip of your tongue against the top of the back of your lower set of teeth. Now, stretch the middle of your tongue out through both sets of teeth. Stretch the middle of your tongue out until you feel your tongue pull at its roots in the back of your mouth. Stretch and loosen those root muscles. Know where they are. Feel them relax after you have stretched them. If you can relax your tongue's root muscles, you can open your throat and you won't choke off sound. You won't swallow sounds or get them stuck in your soft palate or adenoid area.

The Jaw

Tension in your jaw will also stop sound from reaching your resonators. To loosen and free your jaw, take the heels of your hands, place them in your cheeks and gently massage your jaw downward away from its hinges. The jaw's hinges are just outside the openings of your ears. It should feel good to massage and loosen up your jaw. Now, take hold of your chin with your finger tips and move your jaw up and down on its hinges. Free it to move easily on its hinges.

The Tongue

The most open articulator sound is "Aaah." To make a pure, resonant "Aaah" sound, not only must you open your throat and relax your jaw, but you must also let your tongue lie flat on the floor of your mouth. If you can't get your tongue to lie flat, rest it on the floor of your mouth and think the sound "Mmm" but don't make the sound. Feel the edges of your tongue spread out and touch the sides of your cheeks. Now, your tongue should be relaxed and lying flat.

Chest Resonation

Let's test an open articulator, low register sound and see if your throat, jaw and tongue are free and relaxed enough to allow the sound to resonate where it wants to. Put your finger tips on your chest. Breathe deeply using your bellows. Say, "Zaa." Relax your jaw, open your throat and let your tongue lie flat. Extend the "Zaa" sound. Take another breath if you need to. Can you feel the vibrations in your chest and hear the mellow, low register sound? If so, you have good woofer or chest resonation.

Girls and some women may have problems producing a full chest resonant sound but "Zaa" wants to resonate in the chest and eventually, if you free your throat, jaw and tongue and focus but don't force the sound to your chest, it will resonate there. You will have begun to develop a good low register vocal tone.

Mask Resonation

For many people, especially men, getting a loud, high register, closed articulator sound to resonate in their masks presents problems. When you try to make such a sound, you may habitually tighten up your throat and jaw.

Make an "Eee" sound. Can you feel the middle of your tongue pressing up against the hard palate? That's what it should be doing. "Eee" is the most closed articulator vowel sound. The tongue is shutting off most of the mouth's cavity that was open when you made the "Zaa" sound. Put your finger tips alternately over your upper and lower sinuses and then the bridge of your nose. Take a deep breath with your bellows. Relax your jaw and your tongue's root muscles. Say "Eee." Extend the sound. Can you feel the sound vibrating and hear it resonating in your mask? That's where it wants to resonate.

Now, make a long, extended, high register — an octave above your normal speaking voice — "Nee" sound. Make it louder. Does your jaw and throat tighten? Is the sound choked off and screechy? There is no excuse for this tension and chocking. You can make a loud, high register "Nee" sound and relax your tongue's root muscles and loosen your jaw by dropping it slightly. Try it again. The sound wants to resonate in your mask, so let it. Don't force it, think the sound into your mask. It may not happen right away, but eventually, if you can get a loud, high register "Nee" to resonate freely in your mask, you can get any sound to resonate there. You can develop a good, high register vocal tone.

If you have felt sound vibrating in your chest and mask and heard it resonating in both places, you know your voice can have tonal variety.

The Hard Palate

Here is an exercise to make sure speech or language gets

articulated and sounded as clearly and strongly as it should. Many women have been urged as young girls to be "ladylike," to speak softly. Consequently, they have problems getting their voices into the front of their mouths where it can be articulated clearly and resonated off their hard palates. They swallow their voices and so do many other people.

Does your voice resonate off your hard palate easily? Take a deep breath with your bellows and hum to your closed lips. To free your lips to work naturally, alternately sneer and pout with them. Stretch your lips by sneering and pouting grotesquely. Flutter your lips as a horse would flutter its lips when begging for a cube of sugar or some grain. "Mmm" loudly and make your lips vibrate. When you have established a good, strong humming sound, open your lips and lower your jaw and let the "Mmm" become an "Aaah." If you are swallowing the "Aaah" sound, try again and relax your tongue's root muscles and drop your jaw from its hinges. Let the "Aaah" sound resonate off your hard palate as well as in your chest.

If that doesn't work, try this. Stand erect. Take a deep breath with your bellows. Make an extended "Zaa" sound and tip your head forward, down your spine. Maintain the "Zaa" sound and tip your whole body down your spine and over your hip joints until you are hanging upside-down. Feel the "Zaa" vibrating out of the top of your head into the floor. Now, upside-down, take a full breath and voice a high register, loud "Hunh" sound. Relax your jaw and open your throat. Feel and hear the sound resonating in your head and mask but especially off your hard palate. Slowly roll your back up and keep voicing the high register, loud "Hunh" sound. As you unbend you should feel the sound in your chest, then your mask, but also in your mouth. Once you are standing erect, move your head gently with the seven neck vertebrae. Take a deep breath and send that "Hunh" sound to your hard palate. Relax your jaw and open your throat. If you can get a "Hunh" sound to resonate off your hard palate, with practice you'll always get your voice into the front of your mouth where it should be. You'll be well on your way to developing strength and clarity of articulation.

Full Resonation

When you can get low register, open articulator sound to resonate in your chest and high register, closed articulator sounds to resonate in your mask and any sound to resonate off your hard palate, you will have realized full resonation potential. Eventually, you can get any vocal sound to resonate in any or every resonator. Low, open sounds resonate best in the chest, and high, closed sounds resonate best in the mask, but every vocal sound can resonate in any resonator you want it to. In fact, when your vocal mechanism is completely warmed up, each sound should vibrate and resonate throughout the whole resonator system. A sound may be stronger in one place than another but all of an open resonator system is open to all sounds.

Once your vocal mechanism is fully resonant, it is also ready to amplify vocal sound, to project your voice.

Amplification and Projection

Let's turn your resonators into amplifiers. Pretend you want to call a taxi three blocks away. You are going to call out "Taax!" "Eee!" You are going to resonate "Taax" from your chest and "Eee" from your mask. Take a deep breath. Plan to take another breath between "Taax" and "Eee." Give each sound plenty of energy but relax your jaw and open your throat. Go ahead, call the taxi. If either sound got caught in your throat, you probably habitually try to use your vocal chords to project your voice. Stop doing that! Use your resonators as amplifiers. Then you won't lose your voice cheering at the big game, and your rich, resonant voice will be heard in any theatre anywhere.

Comments and Suggestions

If you haven't been able to do what I have asked you to do with your voice, you might read through this section again and take more time with each of my suggestions. If, however, after a few tries, my suggestions still don't work for you, then you need voice lessons. To become a fine actor, you must free your natural voice and attain the tonal variety, articulation and amplification necessary for full vocal expression. Read Kristin Linklatter's *Freeing the Natural Voice*. Find a vocal production teacher who believes in the natural process. Take singing lessons even if you don't have problems with vocal production. What I have said about dance lessons applies, of course, to singing lessons: to get a part in musical theatre, you have to be able to sing, dance and act.

If someone who you think pronounces words well tells you that you pronounce words strangely, maybe he means you have a different regional accent than he has. Maybe, however, he is hearing you use your articulators improperly. Maybe your teeth are getting in the way of your tongue or maybe your jaw or your lips aren't working properly. Check with a voice therapist.

Standard Stage Speech

I don't think every actor should cultivate Standard Stage Speech. Many successful, good actors have maintained their regional accents. It is part of what is distinctive about them. They are also, however, the kind of an actor who usually plays one type of character rather than playing different characters with different dialects. If you want to be a complete actor, an actor who can create different voices for the different characters you will create, you need not only to free your natural voice but to learn to use Standard Stage Speech. Creating a dialect is a matter of using your ear for the sounds of language and making specific changes in Standard Stage Speech.

BODY ALIGNMENT

What Is It?

I have suggested some physical exercise for warming up and limbering up the limbs and joints of your body. Now, I want to help you get your limbs and joints balanced. Knowing how to balance or align yourself when you are standing, sitting or moving is important. First of all, an aligned body has both strength and relaxation. In times past, members of the aristocracy were taught to stand, sit and comport themselves in alignment. They recognized that a person with an aligned body expressed the combination of assurance and relaxation a member of the ruling class should express. Also, alignment is the body's natural posture and the position in which an actor can breathe, speak and move at his best. It is not only your natural posture, it is a neutral position to which you can make specific changes when building the physical aspects of a character who is specifially different from you. You may not be aware of it but, more than likely, your body is habitually out of alignment. Your posture has probably made adjustments to social and psychological pressures. Parents or the military may have persuaded you to stand straight or at attention. Girls often are told to hold their shoulders back in order not to slouch. One person may unconsciously express the desire to hide from society by ducking his chin. Another person may unconsciously express the desire to confront or rise above society by thrusting his chin forward.

If you are out of alignment anywhere, the secret is to gently think yourself into alignment section by section. Don't try to force anything to happen. Your goal is to establish a relaxed body as well as an aligned body.

Standing in Alignment

Dress in a leotard or get naked and stand in front of a mirror. Relax and stand as you normally stand. Face the mirror. Put your feet underneath the outside of your shoulders and flat on the floor. Feel your toes, heels, and both sides of each foot touching the floor. Look in the mirror. Is there more weight on one hip joint than the other? Is one shoulder riding up? Balance the weight of the trunk of your body on both hip joints and watch the shoulder that was riding up come into line.

Turn sideways to the mirror. Imagine a plumb line, a string with a lead weight attached at one end, hanging from the top of the middle of your skull down through your body with the lead weight hanging free between your feet. Except for a natural concave curve in your back, your body should align itself without any tension along this plumb line.

Your feet, as before, should be underneath the outside of your shoulders and flat on the floor. If that seems uncomfortable or you feel as if you are going to fall over backward or forward, have patience. You are out of alignment somewhere. When you get into alignment and get used to it, you will be able to stand comfortably with both feet flat on the floor.

If your knees are locked, unlock them. If your butt is sticking out and you have tension in the small of your back, don't force it but think your pelvis forward gently.

If your lower tummy is thrust forward, think your pelvis backward. If your upper stomach is protruding, think your rib cage back.

Let your arms have the weight of gravity and hang at your sides. As your arms hang easily at your sides, move your head gently using the seven neck vertebrae. Feel any tension in your shoulders being released.

If your chin is ducking under or jutting forward, think it into line.

If you have made all the adjustments you needed to make and maintained them, you are now standing in alignment. If you were uncomfortable standing with your feet flat on the floor, you should now feel more comfortable.

Advice

If you are uncomfortable standing in alignment, keep practicing and you'll get used to it. It is the way the body wants to support itself. If you continue to be uncomfortable establishing alignment, you need a specialist's help. Seek out an Alexander Technique*-accredited teacher. He or she will give you a hands-on course that will bring your body into line. You will enjoy the process.

T. Matthias Alexander, The Man and His Work (see Bibliography)

Sitting in Alignment

To sit in alignment, let the trunk of your body rest against the back of a straight-backed armless chair. Feel your butt bones, the backs of your hip joints, supporting the trunk of your body. Feel your thighs resting on the seat of the chair. Put your feet flat on the floor. If your feet don't reach the floor, put a stack of books or a telephone book or two under them. Let your arms hang at your sides. Move your head gently using the seven vertebrae that support it. Feel any tension in your shoulders release itself. You are sitting in alignment. You should feel strong and relaxed at the same time. You should be able to breathe deeply and easily using your bellows.

Actors Equity, the actors' stage union, requires that management provide enough straight-backed chairs offstage for each of the actors who wait offstage for his or her cue to go on stage. You will always have a straight-backed chair available in which to sit and relax and prepare for your entrance. You should learn to use it, to establish the relaxation and concentration an actor needs before he or she goes to work in a class or a rehearsal or a performance.

Walking in Alignment

If you can stand in alignment, you can walk in alignment. Simply get into alignment and then let your legs swing forward from your hip joints. Let the weight of your body roll forward on your heels to your toes. As you move forward, maintain alignment in your upper body. Let your arms swing naturally. There's nothing more to it.

When you can stand, sit and walk in alignment, practice doing it in everyday life. Make a habit of it and your body will feel more relaxed and assured than it has ever felt.

Sit in alignment in a straight-backed chair without arms. Close your eyes. Let your arms hang heavily at your sides. When you have attained as much physical relaxation as possible decide on a specific outdoor place where you would like your mind's eye to take you. (Acting class, Providence, Rhode Island.)

3. RELAXATION

PHYSICAL RELAXATION

Actors' Energy or Nervousness?

Lee Strasberg once said during an Actors Studio class that he thought that good acting technique is fifty per cent relaxation and fifty per cent concentration. I believe that there is a third element to the formula and that is the actor's energy, that extraordinary energy that comes with the excitement of giving a performance. The relaxation-concentration process is a method of controlling that energy and putting it to creative use.

The prospect of creating multidimensional human life on the stage or in front of a camera is thrilling but the anticipation of doing it in public often brings mental anxiety and physical tension to the actor. Physical tension in any form bottles up an actor's energy. If a bottle of champagne is shaken and left corked up, the bottle may explode. If the bottle is shaken and quickly uncorked, its contents will flow all over the place.

Give an actor a good part and more than likely he gets all shook up in nervous anticipation. Well-trained actors learn to trust their nervous energy. They know how to transform their nervousness into useful energy. They relax and concentrate their energy into what their character is thinking, feeling or doing. Inexperienced actors, on the other hand, are often frustrated by nervousness. They keep nervous energy corked up until they feel like they are going to explode, or they pop the cork too quickly and their energy flows all over the place.

Actors' Tension or Your Character's Tension?

So that you can concentrate energy and not bottle it up or dissipate it, you should always bring as much physical relaxation to your acting as possible.

When physical tension occurs in class or in front of an audience or a camera, don't argue with yourself about whether it is actors' tension or character tension. Learn to relax and stay in character at the same time. No matter how different your character's personality is from yours, he or she wouldn't want to live with tension any more than any human being would.

Physical tension in any form frustrates human expression. If emotion is welling up inside you, tension will inhibit or distort your expression of that emotion. Don't put up with tension in a theatrical situation any more than you would put up with it in everyday life. It will either stop you from doing an actor's work or force you into overacting.

The Quick Physical Relaxation Method

There is a quick way to release physical tension and stay in character in the midst of an audition, a rehearsal or a performance. You can keep doing what you're doing and saying what you're saying and at the same time move your head gently using the neck's seven vertebrae. Feel the tension in your shoulders release itself. Let your arms have weight. Breathe deeply with your bellows and let out a sigh. Suddenly, you will think clearly, feel deeply and behave freely again. You will come back to life as a creative actor and the character you are playing or creating.

Physical Relaxation in Preparation to Go to Work

I teach my students a specific physical relaxation process that should work for you. The first time I have my students do the exercise, I have them lie flat on their backs on the floor, their heels, legs, arms, hands, behinds, shoulders and heads resting on the floor.

I ask them to pretend that they are being stretched on a rack. With their arms extended above their heads, I have them imagine that their wrists and ankles are strapped to a table and the table is going to separate under their behinds, stretching their toes away from their finger tips. The table opens an inch each time I clap my hands. Once they have achieved the ultimate in physical tension, I tell them that their straps are released and they should place their arms at their sides and begin to give in to the gentle pressure of gravity.

I suggest that they gently close their eyes and let their whole body — head, shoulders, behind and limbs — melt into the floor. I suggest that they are at the beach lying in the warm sand. I ask them to feel the cool breeze and the warm sun on their faces, hands and tummies. I say to them:

Think of the skin on top of your head not as a drum skin or a tom-tom skin, but as a nice, loose nylon net. The edges of the net, behind your ears, at the top of your forehead and at the nape of your neck, could just flip-flop in a breeze. The skin on your forehead is loose and your eyebrows hang from the loose skin on your forehead. Your cheeks are loose and hang from your cheekbones. Feel the warm blood flowing gently from under the loose skin on top of your head, down under the skin on your forehead, around your eyes and under the loose skin of your cheeks.

If I see tension in their foreheads or their eyebrows or under their eyelids, I ask them to imagine dark blue velvet in front of their eyes.

Once I see that all their facial muscles have relaxed, I ask them to loosen their jaw hinges, yawn deeply and sigh an extended sigh. I tell them to breathe gently and deeply using their bellows. When I see that their stomachs are contracting and expanding naturally and easily, I know that they have achieved total physical relaxation.

I then bring them back to life by suggesting that the earth's energy is pouring up from the floor underneath them. I suggest that their inner energy will support their bodies and allow them to levitate about three inches off the floor. When I see energy pouring back into their bodies and the pressure of gravity being released, I know they are relaxed without being enervated. I have them sit up, keep their eyes closed and consider the extent of their relaxation. Any vestige of tension has to be the product of mental anxiety.

Too Much Energy

The relaxation exercise I just described is designed to relieve your everyday physical tension and allow you to begin to concentrate your very special actor's energy. This physical relaxation exercise should be preceded by a set of muscle warming up and joint loosening exercises. If, after the warming up and loosening exercises and the physical relaxation exercise, you still feel fidgety and hyperactive, go run around the block a few times. Too much energy can inhibit physical, facial and vocal expression as easily as tension can.

MENTAL RELAXATION

Actors' Anxiety

If the source of your tension is mental anxiety, there are specific ways to calm that anxiety before it expresses itself physically. Mental anxiety is most often a preoccupation with failure. When I was a young actor my need for a job often became my biggest obstacle to getting that job. Walking into the inner office of a Madison Avenue advertising agency to audition for a television commercial that could make me thousands of dollars was like walking into a torture chamber.

Acting courses had taught me nothing about how to deal with mental anxiety. Psychiatric therapy might have helped but I never found the time or the money for it. When I wanted to stop smoking, however, I went to a hypnotist. He didn't help me stop smoking but his mental suggestion process introduced me to a technique that releases mental anxiety for almost everybody, at least temporarily.

Because this method uses sense-memory to get your mind to dwell on pleasant images, it will fit right in with the actors' technique you are learning. The use of sense-memory concentration is the focus of Stanislavsky's *The Actor Prepares*.

When I learned to control mental anxiety and I had more experience auditioning and more actors' technique to depend on, I took advertising agency auditions for commercials in stride. More often than not, the agency's inner office became a funhouse. I averaged three class A commercials a year. Selling paper towels, beer, candy bars and soap on TV paid for the opportunity to work off-Broadway, where in my day, the minimum salary was around sixty dollars a week. Without learning to release mental anxiety, however, I don't think I would have developed the actors' technique that made it possible for me to get jobs in commercials, off-Broadway, on Broadway and in movies and television.

Sitting Down to Relax

The first step in releasing mental anxiety is to establish physical relaxation. When I teach my mental relaxation exercise, I have my students physically relax sitting rather than lying down. I advise them that lying flat on their backs is the most reliable way to gain thorough physical relaxation but there may be times when they feel self-conscious about doing this. Sitting down in public to relax is less obtrusive than lying down. There are always those Equity chairs I told you about ready for you offstage. With practice, you can relax as thoroughly sitting down as lying down and there is less chance of your becoming enervated and having to regenerate your energy.

A Mental Relaxation Exercise

As I have taught you, sit in alignment in a straight-backed chair without arms. Close your eyes. Let gravity press the trunk of your body into the seat and against the back of the chair. Let your feet rest flat on the floor or on books on the floor in front of you. Let your arms hang heavily at your sides. If, during the exercise, your hands begin to fidget, rest them in your lap.

When you have attained as much physical relaxation as possible, decide on a specific outdoor place you know well where you would like your mind's eye to take you. Your mind's eye is what allows you to see, with your eyes closed, what you are thinking about. Make your place a relaxing, comfortable place where you have been content, happy and at ease. Sitting in alignment, maintaining physical relaxation, with your eyes closed, you are going to remember your way to this place with your mind's eye.

Even if the place is near where you live, don't let your memory rush to that place. Take your time and let your mind's eye see your way there. Remember the turns and the unders and overs. Remember the landmarks. See the size, shape, color and texture of what is along the way. It is a lovely day.

When you have arrived at your place, imagine yourself sitting down there. With your mind's eye, look all around you and find out if everything is where it should be. Take in all the pleasant images. Take your time and see if you can hear, feel, smell and taste what is there.

Explore your place with all five senses and find the most pleasant experience. Indulge yourself; dwell on that pleasant experience until you feel at ease, comfortable and relaxed. As your mind relaxes with its pleasant memories, feel your physical relaxation increase.

If your mind is filled with specific pleasant images, there is no room for anxious thoughts and no chance for mental anxiety to result in physical tension.

When you feel you are ready, open your eyes and look around. See the actual place where you are. Close your eyes again and consider the extent of relaxation you have attained. This is how relaxed you should be before you go to work as an actor.

Always Prepare the Instrument

Physical warming up and limbering, vocal warm-up, and physical and mental relaxation eventually should be combined into one set of prepare-for-actors'-work exercises. You should spend only as much time on each step of the series as you need to, but you should do the exercises in the order I have given them to you. Eventually you should be able to complete the whole set inside of twenty minutes.

I am often asked if an actor should do a set of prepare-to-work exercises every time before he goes to work. My answer is, "Yes.

The actor's instrument is himself. If you aren't given time in the classroom, studio, rehearsal hall or theatre to prepare that instrument for work, do it before you get there."

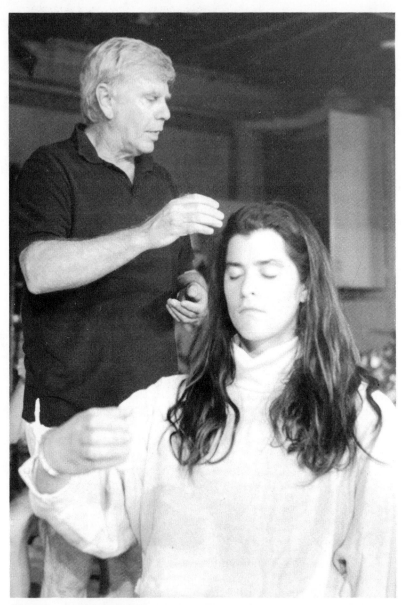

The "Orange Juice" Exercise — Physicalization. With your eyes closed and using your inner sense-memory, recreate the glass or mug out of which you would drink orange juice. (Acting class, Providence, Rhode Island.)

4. CONCENTRATION

Concentration is the term most often used to describe what the actor does to involve himself in an imaginary, dramatic situation. The word concentration is almost interchangeable with the word technique. Concentration is the key to what an actor does while studying, rehearsing, auditioning or performing.

SENSE-MEMORY AND CREATIVE IMAGINATION

What Is Actors' Imagination?

Good acting is dependent on the extent of the actor's ability to pretend to be an imaginary character, living an imaginary life, in an imaginary world. Without getting too philosophical about it, I think it is fair to say that an actor's imagination is not inspiration sent magically from an unknown source. The Romantics may have believed this but I don't think you do. If you do, there is nothing I can teach you.

I believe an actor's creative imagination is a selection of the actor's experiences and memories put together to build the memories, thoughts and feelings of the character he is creating. Take for example Hamlet (in Shakespeare's *Hamlet*) or Electra (in either Sophocles' or Euripedes' *Electra*).

Hamlet or Electra Can Be You

If you haven't lived Hamlet's or Electra's life, you can't pretend to have had the life experiences they have had. You can pretend, however, that Hamlet or Electra have had some of the experiences you have had in your life, experiences that fit logically into the given pattern of their lives.

You may have to broaden your experiences and do some specific research, but with very little effort you will be able to find an experience you have had that is the equivalent of an experience the character you are creating might have had.

Without moving out of the circle of our families we can all recall experiences that range all the way from the glorious to the abominable. Not everyone has seen the ghost of his father as Hamlet does, but all of us have had nightmares in which we saw a loved one in deep trouble. You may not have had a father like Electra's who commanded a great army and who sacrificed your sister to the gods and a mother who killed your father. We all have parents, however, who have done some things of which we are proud and other things that shocked and shamed us.

Sense-Memory, a Creative Tool

You have a storehouse of memories to use as an actor. Every moment of every day more memories are added to that storehouse. Our most poignant memories are not abstract thoughts; they are sense-memories. Our eyes, ears, nostrils, taste buds and nerve ends implant images in our brains. Those images are never lost. When your sense-memory is tuned, you can recall each and every experience you have ever had, and see, smell, taste, touch and hear what you saw, smelled, tasted, touched and heard at a specific time in your past.

A Wealth to Spend in Your Acting

Sense-memory is your most valuable actor's tool. Taking for granted that you include sense-memory experiences of books you have read, movies and plays you have seen, music you have heard, and museums and galleries you have explored, think what a great wealth you have to spend in your acting.

If you feel your life hasn't been full enough to call upon as the creative artist you want to be, get going. If you can't travel and, like many young people, you don't want to read, use the electronic equipment modern society offers you. All of civilization is at your finger tips.

By experiencing again moments you select from your sense-memories, you will be able to create moments in the life of the character you are playing. You can recreate the experience and depend upon the fact that your reaction to that experience, because it is yours as well as the character's reaction, will be an honest, believable, interesting, human reaction, not an indicated or demonstrated reaction.

Tuning Your Sense-Memory

You can make your sense-memories live inside of you or you can project them outside of you. For most people there is a screen just above and in back of their eyes where they can see specific moments from their past. We usually call it our mind's eye. You used it during the mental relaxation exercise to take a trip to an outdoor place.

With practice you can place that screen anywhere outside of yourself that you want it. You will be able, for instance, to look out over the audience or into the camera lens and see a view you have seen from a mountaintop.

Test yourself. Sit in alignment and relax. Close your eyes and remember an object or a section of that outdoor place where you went to relax. See the image projected above and behind your eyes.

Open your eyes and let the image project itself out in front of you. If the image doesn't project, close your eyes and restore the image on your interior screen. Relax, open your eyes and see the same image you saw inside projected out in front of you.

Keep practicing; you'll soon be able to see sense-memories on the interior screen both with your eyes closed and open and, with your eyes open, the same images projected outside of you.

If you can't see the image clearly, you can use one or more of your other senses to bring your memories alive. With your eyes open, remember a favorite person by feeling the touch of his or her hand on yours. Take your time. Taste his or her kiss on your mouth. Smell his or her fragrance. Listen to his or her voice. If you can bring a memory alive with one sense, with practice, you can bring memories alive with all your senses.

Practice using your sense-memory in a class and as homework. Take the time to tune it up. Remember, relaxation is essential to concentration.

FORMING A GROUP

I have been writing directly to you, the beginning actor, and you the experienced actor who may be ready for some retraining. I hope you have been doing the exercises I have described to you. So far, you should have been able to do, by yourself, all the exercises except the Clown Faces exercise.

For this additional work you must form a group of at least four people. You will work together on the remaining exercises in this section. You are going to need a partner for some of the work and you are going to need feedback from your fellow student actors.

Because the actor's work you will be doing is a recreation of the experiences of actual life and because you are going to allow your face, voice and body to express themselves in reaction to the human experience of the actor's work you will be doing, you will not be concerned with how you are expressing yourself while you are expressing yourself. After doing your actor's work you will want to know if your work resulted in believable, multidimensional human expression. Your fellow student actors who have been watching you work will be able to tell you where and when that happened and where and when it didn't happen. Also, you will be able to find out how relaxed and concentrated you seemed to be to those watching you.

Introduce your friends to this book; form a group and keep on working.

The ideal space for your group to work in would be a twenty-by-twenty-foot space at least half of which could be cleared as a work area. The only furniture you will need is a straight-backed chair for each member of the group, a couple of extra straight-backed chairs and a sturdy table approximately five feet by three feet.

Tuning Your Sense-Memory in Class

I have my students practice sense-memory concentration exercises three or four at a time sitting in alignment in front of the rest of the class. They begin each concentration with their eyes shut. When their sense-memory has isolated a specific object, they open their eyes, project the image, and explore the object with all their senses. They recall pleasant and unpleasant objects. They isolate the strongest sense of that object. When they are confident that they can isolate separate objects and explore them thoroughly, I have them sit quietly with their eyes open and remember a whole event from their lives projected out in front of them. Within the sequence of that event, they isolate and explore each and every person, place and thing.

I ask them to project images up and out in front of themselves. This will make sense-memory experiences available to those watching, as described below.

FACIAL EXPRESSION AND BODY LANGUAGE

The students watching the work are witnesses to the fact that relaxation enhances concentration. They comment on the extent of relaxation and concentration they have seen. They also realize that the pleasantness or unpleasantness of a sensory concentration is reflected in facial expression and body language. They let their fellow students know if their sense-memories were reflected in facial expressions and whether they had focused on images far enough out in front to carry across to those watching. They learn that making faces to express pleasure and displeasure is one thing and having a sensory experience and allowing their face and body to express themselves is another thing. Making faces seems false and forced. Facial expression that is an organic reaction to a human experience has truth and dimension.

The students doing the work realize that thorough sensory concentration is dependent on isolating specific objects, people, and sections of places while exploring the specific with all their senses. They come to realize that the strongest sense of a pleasant or unpleasant sensory experience may be trusted to reflect itself clearly and believably on their faces. They find out which of their five senses has the strongest, most dependable memory. They become secure in the fact that sense-memory experiences are available with their eyes open. They are not distracted by being watched. They want to focus their sense-memories at a level out in front of themselves at which those watching will be aware of the pleasantness and unpleasantness of their experiences. They welcome constructive reactions from their fellow students.

Reinforcement Before Criticism

I make it a rule in my classes that, before you tell a fellow student what he did wrong, you must tell him about something he did right. Comment, whether it is called feedback or criticism, is often tough to take. Most people who want to become actors are sensitive and vulnerable. These qualities will help them become fine actors but not if the atmosphere in which they are learning is constantly negative.

We can learn from our mistakes but we can learn even better from what we do right. It is a happier situation when what we do well is reinforced with acknowledgement and praise. Then we aren't on the defensive all the time. We are prepared to accept criticism with a positive attitude.

STORYTELLING

Putting Sense-Memories into Words

Over the years, one of the most popular exercises in my classes has been "Tell a Story." I use it to introduce students to the process of connecting words to sensory experience. The students like the exercise because it helps them to get to know each other. I ask them to tell personal stories about interesting events, trips or people and to begin at the beginning, take their time and remember the details of what happened. They are to recreate the experience of each person, place and thing they remember clearly, and to verbally convey to us what they are experiencing again.

To free the voice to express itself fully and naturally, a vocal warm-up should precede the exercise. While telling their stories, students stand up, sit in a chair or on the floor, or perch or lean on a table. I urge them to find as comfortable a position as possible and to change position whenever they want to. I encourage them to let vocal and physical expression take care of itself. After an extended period of silent sense-memory practice, the results can be surprising.

After a number of stories have been told and we have specific work to refer to, we discuss vocal inflection, gesturing, and eye-to-eye contact. Because the students have already convinced themselves that organic facial expression is preferable to phony, mechanical facial expression, they quickly recognize the difference between phony vocal expression and vocal expression that is connected to a specific sensory experience.

A Quick Test

You can test the difference for yourself right now. Say the phrase, "This is truly wonderful." Say the phrase the way you think it should sound to impress a listener with the wonder of something or other but not anything specific. Make the phrase sound "wonderful."

Now use your sense-memory to remember something specific that is truly "wonderful." Reduce your experience to your strongest sense of this "wonderful" memory. Relax. Stay connected to the experience. Don't care how the words sound. Say again, "This is truly wonderful." Hear the difference?

Coloring Words

When you try to make your voice sound the way you think it should sound to give expression to the words being said, you are coloring your words. Coloring words is a form of demonstrational acting. With very little experience students listening to stories and students in the midst of telling a story can hear the difference between words that are colored and words that are connected to a specific sensory experience. Colored words sound phony and theatrical. Words that are connected to a personal experience sound like human conversation.

Gesturing

Many people, sometimes unconsciously, restrain their hands from making the gestures that it would be natural for them to make.

They may have been told that ladies and gentlemen don't gesture as they speak. They have been misled; if it is natural to them, ladies and gentlemen do gesture when they speak. Other people have taken elocution courses in which they have been taught to make phony, mechanical gestures to emphasize the important points in their speeches.

If you restrain yourself from gesturing with your hands or you make mechanical gestures of emphasis, you are cheating yourself.

You are learning to create believable, multidimensional, human characters. If you allow yourself to make the gestures that are natural to you, you can always adjust them to fit the personality of the character you are creating. Then you will be making adjustments to human expression, not imposing phony, theatrical gestures on yourself and your character.

Eye-To-Eye Contact

When some people tell stories, they easily and naturally make eye-to-eye contact with their listeners. Other people are too shy to do this or they have been told not to do it. I explain that, to bring a story alive, a storyteller should be alternately aware of two things: his reliving of what had happened, and the people with whom he is sharing what had happened.

You don't have to stare at people or lock your eyes to theirs, but if you can make eye-to-eye contact with your listeners, you will know whether you are sharing your experiences with them. You will know whether the descriptive words you are using fit the experiences you are having. You will work moment to moment to convey your experiences clearly. You will become a good storyteller. Almost every character in every play written tells a story. Think about it. Even the secretary who has one line about somebody telephoning and leaving a message is telling a story.

A Story I Will Never Forget

A man, a member of my class, sat in a director's chair and told us about his crash landing an Army glider during the invasion of Germany in World War II. He began by telling us the details of what led up to the landing. It was clear that he was uncomfortable, perhaps about his choice to relive a bad experience, perhaps about his being the center of our attention. His voice was muffled; his feet fidgeted; his hands kneaded the arms of the chair.

As he told about the glide into the landing area, however, he obviously connected to the sense-memory experience. His feet moved gently as he told about working the control pedals. His hands relaxed; his voice was clear. Both his voice and his hands expressed themselves in relation to what he was telling us. His eyes were focused on the landing field ahead of him, in which, he told us, the Germans had sunk telephone poles upright in the ground at twenty-yard intervals.

Obviously, the Germans had been warned about the landing. Our storyteller's glider was one of hundreds and the Germans knew when and where they were scheduled to land. They had booby trapped the field with telephone poles and land mines. They were waiting at the edges of the field with machine guns. A safe landing was impossible and it was too late to land anywhere else.

The storyteller relived the crash and we experienced it firsthand. He felt the shattered windshield and the dirt smash into his face. The storyteller sat back and stopped talking.

As it turned out, miraculously, he was barely hurt. A member of the underground heroically rescued him from the glider.

The storytelling experience does not have to be anywhere near as dramatic as this story was for it to have value. The lesson to be learned from the telling of this story is that, if you relax and take your time and let your sense-memory lead you, your voice, face, hands and body will come alive. They will tell the story in free association with your reliving what happened. Storytelling teaches you that, with sense-memory, you can bring experiences from your past back to life. You can relate to those experiences from your past and react vocally and physically to them as if they were happening in the present.

PERSONALIZATION AND SUBSTITUTION

As you tell your story, you probably will bring a number of people back to life. Personalization is simply the use of a sense-memory of a person. Implicit in the term, however, is the use of substitution.

One way to use personalization is to substitute someone you, the actor, personally know or have known for a person the playwright has your character talk about.

Another way to use personalization is when the actor or actress with you on the stage or in front of the camera doesn't live up to what you believe his or her character should be. It is difficult to flirt with someone who repulses you. Maybe you are going to have to make a sense-memory substitution for that actor or actress. Maybe you are going to have to look at the inadequate actor or actress and see someone you know who does live up to what you believe the character should be. But, don't be too quick to make a substitution. If you make the effort, you will probably be able to find something attractive about the person who first repulsed you. For instance, if you concentrate fully on somebody's lovely voice, you can forget what is unattractive about that person.

Substitution must be used when the playwright has your character refer to a place, object, or event about which you have no sensory knowledge. We have already talked about substituting your experiences for the experiences of Hamlet or Electra.

Blanche Can Be You

Here's another example. Blanche (in Tennessee Williams' *A Streetcar Named Desire*) has witnessed the horrible death of her young husband. She describes in detail what happened.

I hope you never have had and never will have the same experience Blanche has had. Suppose, however, you were playing Blanche and you had to tell the story about her husband's death. You would have to make a substitution.

You may have seen a pet of yours run over. You may have witnessed a bad automobile accident. You may have recently had a horrible nightmare you can remember clearly. You may have seen an event in a movie that affected you as strongly as Blanche might have been affected by her experience. One of these experiences of yours might be the experience you could substitute for Blanche's experience.

If you concentrate on your memories and, at the same time, tell Blanche's story with believable, human expression, no one will ever take the time to judge which experience was more horrible, yours or Blanche's. At least for the moment Blanche will be you.

Now that you are thoroughly experienced in bringing sense-memory alive, you should be able to find substitutes in your storehouse of sense-memories for most of life's experiences. If you feel you are too inexperienced with life, take the advice I have already given you. Get going and investigate more fully what life has to offer. Plays, movies, museums and galleries will do nicely when firsthand experience is unavailable.

Remember, in order to make a sense-memory substitution a powerful and dependable experience, you must explore that memory with all your senses and find out which one of your senses gives you the strongest reexperience of what you are remembering.

PHYSICALIZATION

The Physical World of the Theatre

Our sensory and emotional relationship with the physical world is an important dimension of everyday life. Inanimate objects seem to have a life of their own. The orange juice container you want to get out of the refrigerator is usually hiding behind the milk container. At least one sleeve of the sweater you want to put on has turned itself inside out. When you need to get in the house hurriedly to go to the bathroom, the last key you find in a bunch of keys is the key you need to open the door.

The perfume someone is wearing or someone's personal aroma may persuade you to want to make love to that person. Second-wind breathing can make the last mile of a jog a delirious pleasure but a headache, a stomachache, or a sprained ankle can turn the run into a tortured experience. A sunrise can inspire you and a heat wave depress you.

The physical life of the actual world has an important influence over you. The physical world of the stage or the movie studio, on the other hand, is, more often than not, fake, dead or missing. People in charge of properties turn sleeves right side out. They put the orange juice or the keys where they are handy and they make liquor out of watered down cola. If the weather in the dramatic story is supposed to be hot, the theatre or the movie studio is cold, or vice versa.

As an actor prepares his part in a play, the actor must not only build a character but also build the world in which the character lives. The actor must not only create the physical world that the scenery and costume designers, property people and light and sound technicians may not have provided, he must bring the physical world that is there at least as sensorially alive as it is in the actual world. If it is supposed to be hot, and it is not, the actor must create the heat. If there is supposed to be liquor in the glass and it is really watered down cola, it is the actor's task to turn the cola into liquor.

What Is Physicalization and Why Use It?

Physicalization is the use of sense-memory to:

1. *Create objects in thin air,*
2. *Give life to fake objects found on stage or movie sets,*
3. *Create specific physical states of being for your character.*

44

In their initial improvisations and scenes, I have student actors physicalize most of the objects necessary to their work. Only the basic furniture is really there. If you have to create the size, weight, shape and texture of things in order to use them, you learn to appreciate those things.

When they have learned to create the entire physical world in which their characters live, when they appreciate how important that physical world is to the sensory and emotional life and the physical behavior of their characters, only then do I encourage them to use real objects. When they use real objects, they don't treat them as dead props but as objects with a life of their own to which their characters can relate and respond.

Use All of Your Senses

In real life we are sometimes not conscious of how many senses we use to relate to the physical world. For instance, we sometimes unconsciously smell, taste and listen to things we are only conscious of seeing and perhaps touching. On the other hand, an actor working in the make-believe physical world of the theatre often listens and sees but forgets to smell, taste and touch. Extrasensory physicalization encourages student actors to take their time to relate with all of their senses to the physical world they create.

Extrasensory Physicalization

Not only do I ask my actors to physicalize all the objects except the basic furniture in their first exercises and improvisations, I also ask them to take their time, to pause once in a while, to stop the action and concentrate with an extra sense, to physicalize with another sense than the one or two they have been using. I call this extrasensory physicalization.

Because they aren't performing but are training to perform, the students aren't obliged to do things at a pace they might be done in real life or at a tempo given them by a director. Not only can they stop and smell the roses, they can also take the time to feel the thorns and taste the blood those thorns may have drawn from their fingers.

Full experience of life is dependent on full awareness of the physical world, awareness for instance of heat and cold and pleasant and unpleasant sounds, odors and tastes. You already know that, if the experience is complete, you don't have to demonstrate how you feel about the experience. Your reactions will take care of themselves.

Specific States of Being

Before they begin to build characters, I ask my student actors to create specific physical states of being, a first step in building a complete character. One by one the students stand in alignment in front of the class and step by step physicalize the physical states of being that answer the questions posed by the following character sketches:

1. *A waitress coming home after serving lunch and dinner to three hundred people:*
   Where is she tired?
   What kind of tired?
   How tired?
2. *A policeman directing traffic in New York City in below freezing weather:*
   Where is he cold?
   What kind of cold?
   How cold?
3. *A debutante in New Orleans serving punch at a garden party in humid ninety-degree weather:*
   Where is she hot?
   What kind of hot?
   Does she sit and walk in alignment?
4. *A man who has just been mugged by hoodlums getting up from the sidewalk and making his way to a phone:*
   Where is he hurt?
   What kind of hurt?
   How badly does it hurt?
5. *A man who has had too much to drink, trying to find the right key he needs to get inside his house to go to the bathroom. He is physically unbalanced:*
   Where is he out of alignment?

The more specific students are about the location of each physical state of being and the more they use specific sense-memories of discomfort and pain, heat, cold and fatigue, the more successful they are at fulfilling the exercise.

A Physicalization Initiation

Soon after a student joined one of his private classes, Lee Strasberg would initiate him into the mysteries of The Method with the "Orange Juice" exercise. He would explain that this was the first lesson Stanislavsky gave his pupils. I do the "Orange Juice" exercise with each student I teach. I use the exercise as an initiation of the student into the process of actors' training that began in Russia at the turn of this century and has become today the foundation for the training given in most acting schools around the world. As you do the exercise, please appreciate the fact that it has come from Constantine Stanislavsky to Lee Strasberg to Carlton Colyer to you. Physicalize your "Orange Juice" in good health.

The "Orange Juice" Exercise

Sit in alignment in a straight-backed chair. With your eyes closed and using your inner sense-memory, recreate the glass or mug out of which you would, in everyday life, drink orange juice.

If you don't drink orange juice every day or you don't like orange juice, do the exercise anyway. You must have tasted orange juice once or twice in your life. Your sense-memory will remember the experience. Also, many of the experiences the characters you create will be distasteful. Life isn't all sweetness and honey. Orange juice is both sweet and sour. It is also many other things. Do the exercise and rediscover the dimensionality of the experience.

You are going to physicalize a glass or mug you use almost every day. Keep your eyes closed but project the mug or glass out in front of you.

It is sitting on the table or counter in your house where it most likely would be when it contains orange juice. It is about three-quarters full. See the size, shape and color of the glass or mug of orange juice.

Reach out and let your finger tips feel the surface of the glass or mug. Feel the texture, the smooth or rough, wet, cold surface. Be sure of its shape. Wrap a hand around it and let your palm feel what the finger tips felt.

When you know the glass or mug is in your hand, keep your eyes closed but pick it up. See it. Create the weight and shape with your hand. Move the mug or glass gently and feel the liquid slosh back and forth. When you know the orange juice glass or mug is in your hand, open your eyes.

If you can't see the mug or glass, don't give up! Keep your eyes open. Feel the mug or glass with your palm and finger tips. Transfer it from one hand to the other. Slosh the juice and listen. Smell the juice. Hold the juice up to the light and see if you can see light shine through it. See the pith if it is there. Finally, taste the juice. Drink it down if you like. Pour it on the floor if you want to but not before you have tasted it thoroughly. Put the mug or cup down.

You have been initiated into the fellowship of Method actors. You have physicalized an object. You have created it in all its dimensions. You have explored an object with extrasensory physicalization.

Physicalization, Not Pantomime

At first much of the work of physicalization may seem to you like mime or pantomime. Mime is an ancient art in which actors of farce portrayed the physical behavior and inner feelings of their characters with exaggerated gestures. Without the use of words, they demonstrated the ridiculous personalities of their clown-like characters.

Pantomime literally means "all mime" and the word pantomime is now used in reference to the work of ancient Greek and Roman farce actors, classical commedia dell'arte actors and modern circus clowns. Today, the word mime is usually reserved for the work of artists like Marcel Marceau and his followers. Mime has evolved a technique of its own. It is taught much like dance is taught and its practitioners use their bodies to create a make-believe world in which they imitate life and try to make the audience believe something is happening when it is not actually happening.

Good mime is fascinating. I have seen five men mime a 220-yard dash in slow motion with "Chariots of Fire" theme music in the background. They strived, struggled and tripped each other. They fought from start to finish. I knew all along that they were running in place but their choreographed mime movements made it look as if they were actually covering ground.

Physicalization of the make-believe world of theatre has nothing to do with mime or pantomime. It is a recreation, not an imitation, of life. It is work done by student actors to help them appreciate how multidimensional and alive the physical world of the theatre can be.

An Example of the Creative Use of Physicalization

I had an experience with a well-trained actress' ability to believe in the imaginary world she physicalized that astonished me and the actress. I was directing a first production of a play in which there was a scene at a stock car track in a town in the deep South in midsummer. We rehearsed and performed in an inadequately heated theatre in Syracuse, New York, in midwinter. During the performance, the audience sat huddled in overcoats, mufflers, gloves or mittens, and hats. The actors wore warm clothes in the beginning of rehearsals, but finally they had to strip down to skimpy summer clothes. We rented kerosene burning heat blowers and warmed up the acting area as much as possible.

I asked the actress wearing a bikini under her overcoat to stretch out on a plank of the bleachers at the track and take a sunbath. We decided exactly from where the sun was supposedly shining. The actress spread out a beach towel, took off her overcoat and began to shiver.

"Create a tube of suntan cream," I suggested to her. She physicalized a beach bag and began to dig through it searching for the tube of cream hiding somewhere underneath all the rest of the pretend objects in her bag. As she began to remove things from the bag to uncover the tube, I said, "Hurry up! That sun will broil you. You don't want to go out on a date tonight with a sunburn."

She found the tube. Actually she created it out of thin air. Except for the beach towel, she was physicalizing all of the objects with which she was working. She started to cover her body with the pretend cream and gestured to another character to spread it on her back. When they had finished spreading cream on the actress' body, both actors wiped their fingers on the beach towel.

For the next five minutes of the scene, she lay down on her stomach and sunbathed and flirted with the character who had put the sun cream on her back. Her words sounded warm and sexy. Toward the end of the scene, she sat up and seductively wiped her body with her towel.

When the scene was over, I brought her her overcoat and bundled her into it. I didn't want her to catch cold. I loved her work and she didn't have an understudy.

"You did a great job but you must be freezing," I said.

"I'm getting cold now," she said huddling into her overcoat.

"I really believed the sun was there," I answered.

"Yeah, so did I. At first I got annoyed because I couldn't find the tube. Then, I was frustrated because I didn't know how to get the stuff on my back. When David rubbed the cream on me though, I really began to flirt with him. I didn't know he could be so gentle. When you told me I might get sunburned, that helped me believe, but I think it was the smell of Bain de Soleil™ that really did it for me. I felt like I was back on the beach in Florida and that's when I decided to lie on my stomach instead of my back. I really felt comfy. I wanted to relax and soak up the sun and tease David. I sat up because I actually began to perspire. I did, no kidding! Fantastic!"

"Keep everything!" I said, "Now you've got the relationship with David and I've got the human behavior and the mood of the scene I was after."

When we added real props to the rehearsal, we put a tube of Bain de Soleil, not some cheap substitute, in the actress' beach bag. The property person always buried it under the other stuff in the bag. Thorough work with physicalization can produce astonishing results.

ACTIVITY

Dramatic Action From the Actor's Point of View: Means-Oriented, Not Result-Oriented

The essence of American theatre is action. Audiences come not to listen to the playwright's words, but to see what's going to happen. It is the playwright's task to create a story line that can come alive with conflict and suspense. It is the director's task to see that the performance has pace and tempo. Directors and playwrights should be result-oriented people. They should know where the action of the play is going and how it is going to get there.

Actors should be more means-oriented than result-oriented. They should try to work moment to moment and forget where the play is going and how it is going to get there.

In the process of training, actors should first learn to bring *themselves* alive in public in a pretend situation and create and build characters later. No matter what character you create, *you* will always be on that stage or in front of that camera and you must learn to come physically alive in that situation.

In your first exercises or improvisations, if you have physicalized the place and the objects in it, the next step is to find an activity. Leave the psychological analysis of a character's personality for later. If you know where you are, what's there, and what time of day and what season it is, then decide quickly what you are doing and do it.

Create and then deal with specific heat or cold or pleasant or unpleasant physical states of being. Physicalize the objects and involve them in an activity.

The actor's only responsibility to the dramatic action of a play or movie is to stay in character and to stay alive. Finding an activity and fulfilling it will not only bring you and ultimately your character alive on stage or in front of a camera, it will also initiate human behavior.

Don't Worry About Becoming Too Busy

It is the director's job to decide if there is too much activity for the dramatic moment involved. It is always better for a director to have too much to work with than too little. He can then make a selection from the work the actor has created. He doesn't have to do the work the actor should be doing.

The Childhood Toy Exercise

I have an exercise I use to persuade students that, without direction or planning what to do, they can create an object, find an activity, and behave in public without self-consciousness, as if they were children.

First, I have the students do a set of actors' physical warm-ups, then I ask them to take an inner sense-memory trip back to when they were four or five years old.

> *Imagine that you are lying in your childhood bed comfy and half asleep. Feel what you have on. Feel the weight and texture of your bedclothes. With your eyes closed, let your inner sense-memory take you for a trip all around your childhood bedroom. Take your time and rediscover the whole room: the furniture, doors, windows, wallpaper, rugs, pictures, playthings — everything.*
>
> *When you find an old friend, a plaything you would like to play with again, keep exploring. You may rediscover another plaything that will capture your attention even more than the first old friend did. You can always return to the object that first captured your attention."*

When I see that students have become physically restless lying on the floor and they probably want to get up and play, I tell them that it is early morning, a weekend. The grown-ups are asleep:

> *Open your eyes. Wake up. Get up and find the old friend you would like to physicalize the most. You are in your childhood bedroom. Work with your eyes open. Use extrasensory physicalization. Look and touch, but don't forget to smell, listen and taste. Bring that plaything alive again and play.*

When I see that everybody is completely involved, playing and perhaps behaving as if they were four or five years old, I tell them:

> *You are no longer in your bedrooms. You are in a day care center or kindergarten and you can play together or not as you please but whatever you do, maintain your playthings.*

If they share playthings, they have to talk in order to let each other know what plaything they have physicalized. If I'm lucky, I have led them to create a noisy chaotic playtime. I sometimes have to stop the exercise because the "children" have begun to fight over toys or the boys are teasing the girls or vice versa.

What the Exercise Teaches

This exercise helps persuade actors that, if they create all 360 degrees of the work space around them, they will never be at a loss for objects to turn into activities. It also demonstrates how quickly the right choice of an object can lead to creative physical activity and human behavior.

Marlon Brando in "On the Waterfront"

In the movie, *On the Waterfront*, Marlon Brando, playing the part of a punch-drunk ex-boxer who now works on the docks in New York City's harbor, walks Eva Marie Saint, a gentle young woman, through a park in Hoboken, New Jersey. Marlon's character is courting Eva Marie's character. They are talking about whether it is better to live in the country or the city. Eva Marie goes to a Catholic college in the country. As they are walking, Eva Marie takes a pair of knit gloves out of her coat pocket and inadvertently drops one of them on the ground. Marlon unconsciously picks it up, sits clumsily in a child's playground swing and puts the glove on one of his knarled boxer's hands. His behavior is a wonderfully simple expression of the innate gentleness and innocence of his unromantic, seemingly insensitive character. It is what Bertold Brecht, the German playwright and director, would have called the perfect geste, the right choice of activity for the dramatic moment.

Marlon, probably without thinking about it, but sensorially aware of his physical surroundings, did what came naturally to his character. With the objects at hand, he created activities that express the unexpected dimensions of his character. I have never heard a serious discussion of this movie among well-trained actors in which this scene was not mentioned.

OBSTACLE

For Every Activity There Is an Obstacle

Arthur Penn, the director of the Broadway production and the movie *The Miracle Worker*, and the movie *Bonnie and Clyde*, said in an actors' workshop I attended, "A good actor creates obstacles for himself." I guess what he meant was that, if what an actor did on stage or in front of a camera was so easy to do that the actor did not have to work to do it, then it wasn't worth doing. There's an obstacle to every human activity. This is one of the things that makes human behavior interesting.

A very dramatic example of the use of obstacle is in the movie

The Miracle Worker in which Anne Bancroft as Anne Sullivan tries to teach Patti Duke, the deaf, dumb and blind ten-year-old Helen Keller, some table manners. When the teacher, Sullivan, tries to make Helen eat with a spoon, Helen grabs at anything and everything at hand and hurls it where she thinks it will hit Sullivan. Sullivan casts every obstacle aside and finally forces Helen to hold the spoon and to eat with it. The fight lasts approximately five astonishing minutes.

Not every obstacle to every activity has to turn into such a dramatic event. The really important obstacles are the everyday ones.

If the water you turn on is exactly the temperature you want it to be, if you don't have to turn sleeves right side out, if you are unaware that the sweat trickling down your back is annoying, you aren't alive as a human being. Also, you may have missed the opportunity of a subtle, creative moment.

Marlon Brando found he couldn't get Eva Marie Saint's glove on so he tossed it aside in recognition of the silliness of what he, a grown-up man, a boxer, courting a lady, was doing.

CREATING DRAMATIC ACTION-INTENTION

Intention: What Is It?

When Stanislavsky's teaching was new to the threatre world, the old-timers used to make fun of the upstart Method Actors. They would say, "You ask them to do the simplest thing and they ask, 'What's my motivation?' " When I was a young actor, I never asked that question out loud because I knew I would get in trouble if I did. I did what I was told to do but I always wanted to know why my character would do that. As I studied my lines, I wanted to know why my character would say that.

After I had studied for a short time with a fine teacher named Michael Eagan, I quickly learned that I didn't have to ask questions out loud. I could ask myself questions and give myself actable answers. I could motivate or give purpose to what I was told to do and what I was given to say. Better yet, I could decide for myself what my character was doing and to what use my character was putting his words. What I had learned to do was to use intention.

When you use intention as an actor's tool, you or your character asks, "Why do I want or need to do something or other?" Or simply, "What do I want or need?" The answer should be in the form of an active verb infinitive.

For example:

QUESTION: *Why do I want to say that?*
INTENTION: *To tease her.*

QUESTION: *Why do I want to move over there?*
INTENTION: *To get away from him and to look out the window.*

QUESTION: *What do I want in this situation?*
INTENTION: *To make love to him.*

When Not to Use Intention

Nowadays, most students learn about intention early in their training. They are, however, often asked to use it before they are prepared to use it. I have been in a class in which, as the first step in their training, two students were asked to get up in front of the class and improvise a dramatic situation in which they were to fulfill a specific intention. They were told, "You want to get out of the house and you want to stay."

Because these students weren't given any extenuating circumstances they floundered around and got lost trying to make up words. They tried to playwright a scene on their feet and off the top of their heads, a neat trick if you can do it.

Finally they were given extenuating circumstances but they were overwhelmed by them and the exercise ended in chaos. They didn't know what you know about fulfilling actors' work. You can't put intention to work in a vacuum and you can't work with given circumstances unless you have practiced that work.

When to Use Intention

You already know how to physicalize objects and specific physical states. You know how to turn objects into activities and how to give an activity an obstacle. You can bring an empty space alive by physicalizing all its aspects and you can behave like a multidimensional human being in that space. If you add intention to your work, your work will take on purpose and definition. You will be doing improvisations.

BASIC IMPROVISATION

At their best, improvisations are make-believe, multidimensional situations brought alive by actors without the written words of a playwright or the moment-to-moment instructions of a director.

Doing improvisations before you know the basics of actors'

work won't teach you the basics, but improvisation can do a very good job teaching you how to put the basics together to develop the process of creating a character and the world in which that character lives.

Through Line of Action, Psychological Objective and Line of Intention

Directors have to be result-oriented. They have to plan and keep track of the through line of action of a script. They have to see that the action of the script progresses through the time span of the script with a tempo and a rhythm that builds dramatically toward the climax of that action.

Actors should be means-oriented. Human beings aren't constantly aware of the rhythms and tempos of their lives while they are in the midst of living those lives. They can't predict or anticipate what's going to happen next. They can, however, make decisions about what they want to happen next.

Actors must decide what their characters want out of life and what they want during the time span of the situation in which they are involved in the script. What a character wants out of his life I think of as the character's "psychological objective." What the character wants during the time span of the script, I call the character's "through line of intention."

If the actor concentrates on what his character wants and not on what is going to happen next or on the tempo and rhythm of the through line of action, he will behave as a human being behaves.

The form in which a script is written — comedy, tragedy, etc. — will present conditions upon which actors must base their choices of intentions, but actors should always play their characters' wants and needs, not the director's sense of the pace and tempo of the through line of action.

If the director asks you to pick up the pace, don't just say your words faster; find a reason to heighten your character's intention. Either let your character *need* what he only *wanted* previously or reduce the size or the importance of the obstacles in the way of your character's getting what he wants. If the director asks you to slow the pace, don't just say your words more slowly; increase the size or the importance of the obstacles in the way of your character's getting what he wants. For every intention and action to fulfill that intention there is an obstacle.

If you have your character think in actors' work terms, he or she will behave like a human being. If you or your character thinks in director's terms, you will be in danger of becoming result-oriented. You will begin to anticipate what is going to happen next and your character won't be able to exist moment to moment.

INNER MONOLOGUE

What your character wants or needs can become an inner monologue. If your character wants to hurt another character and you have your character keep saying to himself, "I want to make that guy suffer! I'm going to get back at him! Just wait; I'm going to fix you!" you are using inner monologue. As long as you maintain this inner monologue you can keep your character focused on his intention. Everything you do will have a specific energy and purpose. Your character will try to find a way to overcome every obstacle put in the way of his intention.

Inner Monologue or Sense-Memory?

I use the term inner monologue only for this inner verbalization of intention. For me, however, inner monologue always alternates with sense-memory images of what my character wants, the object of his desires, or what happened to make my character want what he wants.

The sensory image may be a stronger driving force for you than a silent verbalization of intention. Sometimes dialogue or what your character is saying out loud gets confused with what he is saying to himself. This can have amusing results. In any case, it is one thing for your character to say to himself, "I want to make love to you," while at the same time saying out loud the playwright's words, "Pass the orange juice, please." It is another thing to say, "Pass the orange juice, please" while remembering the taste of his or her kiss or the warmth of his or her hand in yours. If inner monologue doesn't work for you, use sense-memory or vice versa.

Choices of Intention and Sense-Memory Are Best Kept As an Actor's Secret

Your sense-memory images should be your secret. Then, you can go as far as you want with them and remember things you might think about but never talk about. You should never have to share your character's intentions or sense-memories with another actor or a director. If the secret is out, everyone will be anticipating what should be happening as you put your memory or intention to use. If you keep your motivations to yourself, no one will know what to expect from you next. Keeping a secret is the biggest attention-getter known to the world of human relationship.

Don't Play States of Being, Descriptive Adjectives, Abstract Thoughts or Complicated Ideas

One of the rules of fine acting is not to play states of being, descriptive adjectives, abstract thoughts or complicated ideas. If you do you will end up indicating or demonstrating what you are doing. Some examples of what not to use are descriptive adjectives or states of being — happy, sad, tired, discouraged, elated, thrilled, etc. — or abstract, complicated ideas like: I want to make myself into a new man; I want to look on the bright side of life; I am going to be a success, find a wonderful woman, put her on a pedestal and worship her for the rest of my life.

To create a happy or sad state of being for your character, have him or her connect with a specific happy or sad experience from your storehouse of sense-memories.

My example of a complicated, abstract idea might be something Happy Loman in Arthur Miller's *Death of a Salesman* might say to himself. What, however, does "wonderful woman" mean? How is the actor creating Hap going to play "look on the bright side of life," "make a new man," "put her on a pedestal?" These are ideas for the actor to put into the back of his mind. They are not playable actions.

Hap is a man whose psychological objective in life is governed by his need to struggle with life. He is a womanizer and a spendthrift. If the actor creating Hap said to himself, "I seem to need to struggle with life. I'm going to stop playing around, work hard and get a promotion in my job, find a woman like Ma and settle down," then the actor would have an inner monologue, a simple set of infinitives that will give a specific energy to what Hap does and says.

The obstacles, by the way, to Hap's intentions are that he dislikes himself and he dislikes his job. Instead of working hard, he makes fun of his bosses. Instead of waiting for the right woman to come along, he tries to conquer every good-looking woman he meets. He has discovered easy, short-term ways to make himself feel better. He has formed habits he can't seem to break despite his good intentions.

BASIC ACTING INFINITIVES

Later, I will discuss the process of establishing a psychological objective in life for a role to be played in a specific movie or play. Here is a list of acting infinitives with which to create intentions or actions, the verbal and physical expressions used to fulfill intentions. Within the list you ought to be able to find just the right infinitive to associate with what you are doing in an improvisation. You can also use the list to find the right infinitive to associate with the words a playwright or a screenwriter gives your character to say. When a writer's words are used as an action to fulfill an intention, then the words will come alive. They will sound like the verbal expression of a purposeful human being. They won't sound like words memorized without purpose from the page of a script.

Basic Infinitives

to baby	to keep away from
to brag about	to make cry
to calm down	to make giggle
to celebrate	to make friends with
to curse	to make fun of
to destroy	to make happy
to discover or rediscover	to make laugh
to drive insane	to make love to
to enjoy	to make smile
to find fault with	to make a lie believable
to flirt with	to pay attention to
to frighten	to pick a fight
to gentle into	to please
to get attention	to praise
to get away	to put in his or her place
to get comfortable	to relax
to get something away from someone	to repair damage done
to get someone to leave or stay	to stay
to have sex with	to support
to humiliate	to teach
to hurt	to tease
to impress	to try to remember
to keep from	to try to touch
	to unburden your troubles

Remember, people don't always want or need to do something to somebody else. They can want to do something to or for themselves.

Also, remember that for every intention a person may have, there is a built-in obstacle to that intention.

Don't Just Stand There...!

It is not enough for the actor to decide which actors' concentration he is going to use. It is not enough to know what your character's psychological objective or intention or inner monologue is. An actor's performance is judged by what he does, not by the technique he used to get it done. What an actor does in performances is to try to fulfill his character's intentions. In order to get what his character needs, the actor has to express himself vocally, physically and emotionally. Physical activities and verbal expressions that are directly related to intention or inner monologue, I call "doings." For every "doing" there is an obstacle, be it ever so slight, to that "doing."

Doing improvisations in an acting class will teach you not only how to make choices, it will also give you practice in putting those choices into action. It will give you practice expressing yourself in character.

An actor doesn't always have to be physically active to be doing something. Your character might be standing or sitting motionless but connected to a strong sense-memory or inner monologue. In that case, the actor is not just standing there; his character is exploring his inner life. The pleasantness or unpleasantness of the experience will express itself in your character's facial expression and maybe vocal inflection and physical attitude.

If the sense-memory experience is focused out an imaginary window or into an imaginary mirror in the space between you and the audience, your facial expression reflecting your feelings about that experience will carry across to the audience. When you connect that experience to a playwright's words, those words will carry your feelings about the experience across to the audience. The farther up and out you focus that sense-memory experience, the farther away, geographically speaking, the person, place or event you are remembering will seem to you and the audience. Of course, if you focus your memories above your head, the audience will think you are connecting to or referring to something in outer space.

All you are expected to do during an improvisation is to work one moment to moment and remain alive by concentrating on the 4 W's you have given yourself. (An outdoor rehearsal of <u>Key Exchange</u>, Brown Summer Theatre.)

5. WORKING WITH IMPROVISATION

Doing improvisational work is an important step in the sequence of actors' training. Doing improvisations will give you the opportunity to practice the process of building a role, a process you will eventually use in your work with a playwright's text. In the mainstream of theatre and in movies and television, improvisation, when it is used, is part of the rehearsal process. You will seldom improvise as you perform. If you become proficient at doing improvisational work, you may someday want to join an improvisational theatre group. Improvisational theatre, however, is a form of theatre all its own.

To become an actor in improvisational theatre you must join a group of actors who have worked long enough together to depend on each other to create a dramatic event in the midst of performing that event. Improvisational actors never build a character. They create characters moment to moment at the same time as they are creating the dramatic event.

They do take dramatic events that have evolved in performances and rehearse them, perfect them, and repeat them in subsequent performances. They never, however, put their work into a written form to be memorized.

A History of Improvisational Theatre

Improvisational theatre of today is part of a great tradition. It has its roots in the improvisational theatre that evolved in sixteenth-century Italy, commedia dell'arte theatre. From the sixteenth century through the eighteenth century commedia dell'arte troupes traveled over Western Europe playing combination farcical-romantic comedies. These comedies were as popular with royalty as they were with the masses.

Like the improvisational groups of today, these troupes worked without a script. Their performances were improvised around a bare outline of a plot, a scenario. Unlike the improvisational theatre of today, each actor always played the same character. The comedians wore character masks and they expressed themselves with pantomime.

The heyday of improvisational theatre in the United States was in the 1950s, '60s and '70s. It began in Chicago, and its most famous groups were The Compass, Second City and The Premise. At their best, the performers could take a phrase shouted from the audience and immediately turn it into a poignant dramatic situation. Many fine actors built their actors' technique in improvisational theatre and then brought that technique into mainstream theatre.

Improvisation in Mainstream Theatre, Television and Movies

Today, plays and movies and taped television shows often strive for an improvisational tone. Moments in movies and taped television may be improvised and moments in plays are often developed out of improvisations done in rehearsal. That doesn't mean, however, that whole plays are developed out of improvisation or that an entire movie or television tape is improvised in front of the camera. The only play I know that was developed almost entirely out of improvisation is *Hatful of Rain*. Its situations and characters were created in improvisations at the Actors Studio and then Michael Gazzo wrote a script based on the improvisations. The actors who created the characters in the improvisations played those characters in the original Broadway production.

Improvisational theatre on television has a very limited history. Much of Sid Caesar's "Your Show of Shows" was improvised both in rehearsal and live on the air. Caesar and his company of actors worked much the same way as actors in an improvisational theatre group would work. Sid Caesar's show, however, was unique. Improvisational theatre on television was over when "Your Show of Shows" went off the air.

The television comedy show "That Was the Week That Was" created a format that "Saturday Night Live" now uses: social satire done live with a company of actors with improvisational theatre backgrounds. The skits on these shows may seem improvised but the actors use written scripts, part of which they have memorized and part of which they read from the teleprompters.

Performances in live theatre and in television and movies that seem to be improvised are often performances in which the words are delivered as if they hadn't been written beforehand. Many good actors can make written dialogue sound as if their characters were finding and using words as the words occur to them, moment to moment.

SOLO 4 W'S (WHO, WHERE, WHEN, WHAT)

Solo improvisations are designed to teach you to depend on yourself. Because there often isn't the time in rehearsal needed to build a framework of human existence and behavior for your character, you will be forced to work alone at home to get the work done. If there is no one to talk to or play off of, you can still build a framework to support the words the playwright has written for your character.

When you first do solo 4 W's improvisations, to explore all the levels available, you will have to consciously change your concentration from one level to another. After doing a few, however, you will find that for the most part the levels will overlap of their own accord. Even when doing your first solo 4 W's improvisations, the levels will occasionally overlap automatically. There are always four levels of concentration that are required to create multidimensional human behavior. They are dependent on each other for existence. When they begin to overlap of their own accord, let them. Allow multidimensional human behavior to happen when it wants to happen.

You will be given a primary level of concentration. When you are in doubt about what to do next, go to your primary level of concentration. Before you begin to go to work, however, define each of the four levels of actors' concentration that are required to create multidimensional human behavior.

The 4 W's Levels of Concentration

WHO: The person you intend to be. Age and occupation will do (see below).

WHERE: Choices of kinds of places will be given later. You must physicalize the specific aspects of the place and the objects there. Use your sense-memories of a place that is similar to the place that will be given. You must also decide where your character has been and where he is going from here. You must create specific sense-memories of where he has been and where he will go later. You must personalize the people he has been with and will meet later.

WHEN: Time of day and season. Create a specific, not a general, weather situation.

WHAT: What your character wants to do in this place. Let activity and "doings" happen moment to moment. Create obstacles to intention and activity.

A Basic Physicalization of Age

Because you aren't as yet creating a specific role, it will be enough, for the purposes of this improvisation, to work on profession and physicalization of age.

Before we do 4 W's improvisations in my classes, we have researched the specific ways different age groups, from children to octogenarians, physicalize their age.

Each student is assigned a different age group. As homework, over an extended period of time they are to observe people in their assigned age group and concentrate on the following things:

1. As they stand and sit and walk, where and how much are they out of alignment?

2. When they move, where is the main source of their energy: toes, hip joints, arms, hands, chest, etc.?

3. Are their limbs and joints loose and lively or stiff and infirm? Where specifically are they loose, lively, stiff or infirm?

Each student is to study enough people in the age group assigned to him or her to try to establish a common denominator of how people in that age group physicalize their age.

In class we share our observations by physically demonstrating what we have learned.

Profession (The Day-by-Day Work Your Character Does)

When you choose a profession for your character, you can realize specifically where physically, because of his work, he would be tired or tense, strong or infirm. You can be more specific about the clothes he is wearing and the objects he might be carrying. If, in improvisations, you physicalize clothes and personal objects, you will have more of an appreciation for the costumes and props you eventually will be given when playing a specific role.

Solo 4 W's Improvisations — Establishing the Place

The biggest similarity between working in improvisational theatre and doing improvisations as part of the training for mainstream theatre is that in both cases the actors work without sets, props and costumes. In both cases the only furniture used are a few chairs and a table. In both cases objects and aspects of the place are physicalized.

In my classes we establish place with only a sturdy, fair-sized table and a couple of straight-backed chairs. The locations we find most useful are public places where an individual would not be out of place doing his own thing:

bus stop	*railroad station*	*park*
airport		*beach*

Malls and markets work less well because activity is dictated by the place and not by the actor's imagination.

The table can be the base of a store's display window, a rock, part of a boardwalk, a baggage carrier, etc. The chairs can double as a bench.

I encourage students to walk their place before they go to work in it. It helps, of course, to make aspects of the place specific sense-memories of a similar place. I ask the students to establish what's there, 360 degrees around them. Sometimes it helps to talk out loud as you walk the place.

> *Here's a bench, grimy. There's a sports store window. Yeah, a sale on sneakers! Here's a curb. The bus would be coming from that direction. Lots of traffic and exhaust fumes. Tall buildings across the street, a park out left. I'm going to come from over here. I just walked six blocks from my office building. Damn! I'm cold.*

That's a place an actor can stay alive in even if his intention is the seemingly passive action of waiting for a bus.

No Further Plans Needed

You aren't to plan what you are going to do or how you are going to do it. Have someone whisper a primary level of concentration in your ear at the last minute.

All you are expected to do during the improvisation is to work moment to moment and remain alive by concentrating on one or more of the 4 W's you have given yourself. When in doubt about what to do, concentrate on the level of work whispered in your ear. You can't leave the place until someone in charge says that the improvisation is finished.

An Example of a Solo 4 W's Improvisation

I recently had a woman student do a 4 W's improvisation of a woman her own age but seven months pregnant searching a park, trying to find the man who had made her pregnant. The student had never been pregnant but she is a nurse in a maternity ward. Her sense-memories may have been secondhand but her physicalizations were specific and therefore truthful and believable.

She made it a humid summer day and she used the discomfort this gave her as an obstacle to her intention, looking for the father.

She had been given a "Where" primary level of concentration so she chose various vantage points in her park from which to look at the passersby. She clumsily climbed a rock and had to call one of the actors watching her work to help her down.

She rested on a bench. Her inner sense-memories of the man for whom she was searching and her inner monologue kept her alive. A combination of the humidity and her unpleasant and pleasant memories and thoughts made her restless. Her facial expressions told the story of the predicament in which she found herself. She got up and cooled her feet by wading along the edge of a pond.

Guessing Games

When the improvisation is over, if your audience uses specific examples from your work to support their guesses, it can be a fun game and a useful exercise for the audience to guess:

How old did you intend to be?
What was your profession?
What time of day or season was it?
Where did you come from and where will you go from here?
What specific objects and activities did you create?
Was the event a pleasant or an unpleasant experience for you?

When you put all the guesses and supporting evidence together, you will know whether the actors' work you did resulted in believable, multidimensional human behavior.

Don't Try Demonstrating or Indicating

Guessing games that encourage the actor to make his audience guess correctly are dangerous. If you feel you need to get the audience to guess correctly you will be tempted to demonstrate and indicate. You will be more conscious of getting results than finding the means to bring your character and his surroundings dimensionally alive.

Remember solo 4 W's improvisations are designed to teach you that you can work alone and create a framework of multidimensional human existence and behavior on which to build a character, a framework to support the words written for your character by a playwright.

ENSEMBLE (RELATIONSHIP) IMPROVISATIONS

Complex Ensemble Improvisations

Basic improvisation is what you do to learn the process of creating a character and building a role.

An example of complex improvisation is the work that was done when the production of *Hatful of Rain* was developed out of improvisation. Complex ensemble improvisations are improvisations based on an idea or a theme to be developed into a dramatic situation, with a beginning, a middle and an end. Eventually the dialogue will be set and the action will be blocked.

I have done a series of skits with fourth grade children. These skits are a study of conflict in children's lives. They are used to help children solve conflict without fighting and hurting each other. First the children give me examples of conflict in their lives: conflict in a family, a classroom, a playground or the street. With suggestions from me, the children improvise dramatic situations from the examples given. We select moments from these improvisations that we can build into a skit with a beginning, a middle and an end. With my direction we rehearse the skits and eventually perform them and videotape them.

Both the children who perform the skits and the children who watch them learn a lot about acting and about positive human relationship.

Basic Ensemble Improvisations — *Learning the Process of Creating Character and* *Character Relationships*

Basic ensemble improvisations that teach the moment-to-moment process of creating a character and character-to-character relationships should not be designed to develop, necessarily, into dramatic situations with a beginning, a middle and an end.

Remember that you are doing these improvisations to practice a process you will later use in building a specific role. When you are doing ensemble improvisations in preparation for a role, it can be useful to find out how your character relates to strangers and how your character relates to characters in the script, but in situations other than those in the script. Both improvisations will help you build the dimensions of a character and his character relationships that could not be built by working within the confines of the script. Ensemble improvisations will help you extend the work you are doing in the rehearsals of the script. They will extend the work you may have done in 4 W's solo improvisations.

If you want to practice an improvisation in which characters meet as strangers, follow the format of the 4 W's solo improvisations. The same public places will work best. Just add people.

If you want to practice an improvisation in which the characters who come together have a given relationship, a relationship that will develop further in the process of the improvisation, then give yourselves a basic relationship, a relationship that would be given if you were working on a specific role in a playwright's script. Work as: husband and wife, lover and lover, brother and sister, business associate and business associate, etc. (When you get more proficient at ensemble improvisations, add more people.)

If the characters know each other, they seem to relate most interestingly in an intimate environment. Let them relate to each other in a kitchen, a living room, a bedroom or an office. Don't, however, put them at a table in a restaurant where they will just sit, eat and talk. Give them a chance to move and to behave physically.

As in all improvisations, don't plan what is going to happen and how it is going to happen. When working on an entire script, a character's intention in a scene will be conditioned by that character's psychological objective in life and his through line of intention in the situation in which he finds himself in the entire script. Because, as yet, you have not developed all the dimensions of your character and you are not working on an entire script, let someone whisper your character's intention in your ear.

Each actor should be given an intention that could conflict with another character's intention. A conflict between characters will bring out the truth of the relationship between those characters.

Don't fool yourselves that a given relationship and given intentions will, by themselves, bring the improvisation alive. You must make 4 W's decisions, decisions about ages, professions, aspects of the place, objects, time of day, season, etc. Of course, when doing ensemble improvisations, the decisions must be made in common. One actor can't be creating cold while the other actor is creating heat.

Words Develop Out of the Life You Are Living

Above all don't depend on conversation to give the improvisation life. Words develop out of the life a human being is living. You want to come away from this improvisation with a better sense of your character's feelings, mental attitudes, physical behavior, and physical mannerisms. It is not enough to develop a verbal relationship with the other character or characters.

Stay Connected to at Least One Level of the 4 W's

As you improvise, stay connected to at least one level of the 4 W's at all times. When in doubt about what to do:

Physicalize objects.

Find activities to fulfill intention.

Let obstacles occur.

Deal with the weather, the time of day, pleasant or unpleasant specific physical states of being, including age.

Relate to where you have been and where you may be going (at least one of the characters should come from somewhere else into the space where the improvisation takes place).

Establish an inner monologue and/or an inner sense-memory.

Above all, keep trying to get what your character wants or needs from the situation. If the levels overlap of their own accord, let them. Allow multidimensional human behavior to happen as it will.

Use Words

Put words to use to get what you want. If a conversation develops, let it develop but *do* as you speak. Don't stop an activity to have a conversation. Don't give up trying to get what you want just to talk. As you are talking realize the reason you are talking:

to make friends	*to flirt*
to tease	*to unburden your troubles, etc.*
to pick a fight	*(see page 58 for a longer list)*

If an extended conversation does develop, don't hesitate to make up stories about your character's life. You can create a past life for your character as you are living that character's life.

What to Learn from Ensemble Improvisations

The first thing to learn is that this is the pattern that improvisations to build a specific role should have.

The next thing to learn is that if you allow a character and character-to-character relationships to develop out of moment-to-moment improvisational work, you will be building interesting, multidimensional, human characters and relationships. If you impose an idea of a character or a relationship on an improvisation or a written dramatic situation, you will end up with a clichéd, predictable character and a relationship that has to be forced into existence.

By doing ensemble or solo improvisations you may find moments that can be scored directly into a script. More importantly, without thinking about it or planning it, you will have established behavior patterns, mental attitudes, inner feelings, and physical mannerisms that will incorporate themselves organically into the building of your character.

Party Improvisations

After you have done enough basic improvisations to convince you of the importance of staying connected to the 4 W's, one of the easiest to set up, and one of the most fun improvisations to do, is a party improvisation. You can use it to help the students in a class to get to know each other better. If this is the purpose of the improvisation, all you have to do is set up the place and let the students know where to find the food and drink they will physicalize. The only rule I have about party improvisations is: "Don't just settle down and talk. Eat, drink, dance, play games, make friends, tease, gossip, etc. Keep remembering you can talk and do at the same time in the pretend world of theatre just as you would do in real life."

If you want to use the improvisation to practice building multidimensional character relationships out of an interesting moment-to-moment situation, all you need to do is establish who is dating whom, who is giving the party, who is a stranger in the midst of friends, etc.

Real music can be important for getting a party going. Real alcohol is unnecessary. I've seen some swinging party improvisations in which all the food, drink or whatever was physicalized.

Do Your Own Work.
Don't Direct or Try to Help the Other Actors.

Doing ensemble improvisations should teach you very quickly that if you disconnect from your actors' work to direct or help another actor or to get that actor to help you, you will be cheating yourself. If your character is trying to fulfill an intention and another actor or character seems to be making things difficult for you, welcome the opportunity that has been presented.

To bring a physical activity alive, you consciously created obstacles to that activity. Don't deny the obstacles to your intention presented to you by another actor; welcome them. Assume that the actor has stayed in character and is pursuing his own intention. If you can't get what you want one way, try another way, but stay in character. If the character-to-character relationship develops into a difficult relationship and you expected it to be an easy relationship, well, so be it. That's life, the multidimensional life you have been trying to create all along.

A Family Improvisation

Recently I set up a complex improvisation with teen-age students about a family getting ready for a stranger's coming to dinner. The student playing the mother was trying to get her family organized for the visit. Her son and daughter began to fight for possession of a bowl of Cheetos™. In character, the mother tried to break up the fight but it continued.

The son began to talk back to his mother. Instead of dealing with the situation in character, the mother decided to change roles and become the improvisation's director.

She said to the boy who happened to have a difficult personality in real life, "Don't keep resisting me like that, Duncan." (We usually use the actor's name for the character's name. It helps actors relate to each other as people, not as preconceived ideas of a character.) "I can't play my part if you won't let me. Stop trying to get all the attention!"

I stopped the improvisation and asked the student playing the mother if she was angry with Duncan, the actor, or Duncan, her son.

"I don't know."

"He's being difficult, isn't he?"

"Yes, he always is!"

"Do you still want to get your dinner ready and your family organized?"

"Yes, I guess so."

"Well, don't stop being angry but, if the improvisation needs direction, let me be the director. Duncan's not out of character. He's being a difficult son. He's going to eat those Cheetos and ruin his appetite for dinner. Deal with it. Try again to get him to give up the Cheetos."

She stepped back into character and said, "Give me those Cheetos!"

Duncan replied, "No, Kris wouldn't give me any. I had to take them away from her and now I'm going to eat them."

"Give me that bowl, young man," she countered holding out her hand. She stared down at Duncan who was sitting on the floor protecting his Cheetos. There was strength and conviction in the way she stood.

Duncan began to speak. Then, he stopped and ate another Cheeto. He looked up at his mother to get her reaction.

She stood her ground, hand out and deadly serious.

Duncan stood up, handed her the bowl and said, "Sorry, Mom."

"That's better, son," replied the teen-age mom. "You and your sister behave yourselves. We've got company coming."

The student actress learned a lesson about ensemble acting.

She learned to stay in character and not to deny obstacles and conflict but to deal with them. We developed a skit to perform out of this improvisation and we kept the Cheetos moment in the skit. Duncan always got his mother angry and the mother always dealt with the situation as a mother.

The moment helped establish, for the actors and the audience, the characters of the mother and the son and the relationship of those characters.

Getting To Know You

I was rehearsing for the role of Jamie in *Long Day's Journey Into Night* by Eugene O'Neill. The director and four of the five members of the cast were members of the Actors Studio. We had been rehearsing calmly and easily. What I didn't get done in rehearsal I was doing as homework. I felt I was beginning to know Jamie.

My love-hate relationship with my father and brother was evolving out of a combination of sense-memories of my own family and the personalities of the two men playing opposite me. Our relationships were developing out of the dramatic situation we were rehearsing and the fact that we were not only working together, we were also having lunch and dinner together. As both Jamie and myself, I had begun to feel smothered by the constant intimacy of our relationship. I felt as though I was getting to know these two men too well and that's just as it should have been. That's the relationship in O'Neill's play.

My relationship with my mother in the play also seemed to be taking care of itself. Vivian Nathan is one of the finest actresses with whom I have ever worked. I believed the character she was creating. My stage mother was beginning more and more to remind me of my real mother. I felt comfortable with Miss Nathan even though I knew very little about her. She always went off by herself to have lunch and dinner. And, after all was said and done, I only had one brief scene alone with her.

In that scene, I sat across the table from her, close enough to imagine I saw that her eyes were dilated with the morphine the playwright told us, and Jamie suspected, she had taken the night before.

I confronted her and said, "Mother, take a look at your eyes in the mirror." I was playing the fact that if she looked away from me, she knew that I had caught her. I had forced her to face her own truth. In previous rehearsals she had always turned away.

In the third or fourth rehearsal Miss Nathan didn't turn away. She looked me right in the eye and said, "I don't know you. How dare you accuse me of anything!"

I thought that perhaps she had begun to improvise because

those weren't O'Neill's words. As I began to stammer some sort of inane reply, she said, "OK, everybody take a break. Everybody out! Carl and I are going to have a talk."

"She's going to have me fired," I thought to myself. "I tried to manipulate her once too often."

Instead of the emotional confrontation that I expected, the lead actress telling the juvenile not to try any more of his intimidation tricks on her, Vivian went across the room and got us both a cup of coffee. She asked me how I wanted mine and served it to me back at the table. She sat down opposite me again and said:

> *You're a good actor. You make me as uncomfortable as hell in our scene and that's probably as it should be, but I keep looking across the table and thinking, 'How dare he talk to me like that as if he were my son. I don't even know him!' Who are you, Carl? Where do you live? What do you do besides act?*

For the next half-hour while the rest of the cast cooled their heels in the hall, Vivian Nathan and I got to know each other. It turned out we lived around the corner from each other in Greenwich Village. We chatted more until Vivian finally said, "I feel better; how about you? Now I won't have a stranger for a son."

"I feel great," I said. "I thought you were going to tell me off and maybe get me fired."

Vivian got up and gave me a big hug and a kiss on top of my head. She called the rest of the cast back in and we started our scene again. When I said, "Take a look at your eyes in the mirror," I found that my inner monologue had changed. I wasn't thinking, "Go ahead, turn away and I've got you." I was thinking, "Damn it, I love you, Ma. Why don't you tell yourself the truth about the morphine you take?"

From then on Jamie's and Mary's confrontation was a moment of truth. O'Neill had given me very few words to say but what I said sounded multidimensional and honest.

I kept hoping Ma would tell me she was ready to face the truth about her addiction. I kept hoping she would get up and give me another hug and a kiss but she never did.

Habitual Relationship

I have told you the Jamie-Mary story to emphasize how important I feel improvising can be to building an intimate relationship. This wasn't a formal improvisation, just two people in the place where their characters lived getting to know each other.

One way to get to know each other is to have coffee together, but why not have lunch? Get away from the play and the rehearsal atmosphere, relax and relate to each other as human beings — not as characters whose lives are limited to the two hours they spend in the dramatic action of a play. If you live together in the play, take each other into your homes. If you can share your real lives, it will make it easier to share your characters' lives.

Once you have begun to know each other, do some homework outside of the set rehearsal time. Set up the place where your characters are intimate with each other and do an improvisation around a normal or habitual day in your characters' lives. Use real objects or physicalization but discover the day-to-day activities those people share. Establish the habitual ways these people relate to each other.

Home Base

Find the area within the space to which each character gravitates. In real life each person in a family or a household usually has a chair to call his or her own. If they eat together, each person has his or her own place at the table.

Doing improvisations like these is one way to work toward the organic blocking of a play. When the characters who are supposed to be familiar with each other and the place in which they live really are familiar with each other and the place, then they will move naturally and comfortably in that place. They may not have to be told where to move.

Physical Relationship

If, in the context of a script, your characters obviously sleep together and make love to each other, it isn't necessary that you have sex with your acting partner but it is your task to build a comfortable physical relationship.

Do a habitual behavior normal-day-in-the-life-of-your-characters improvisation, but let yourselves touch each other; hold hands; sit in each other's laps. Give each other a shoulder and back massage while you are waiting around during a rehearsal. Every actor worth his salt can give a good shoulder and back massage.

Of course, you may become attracted to each other. But you will have to deal with that on your own time. You won't find what to do next in the actors' work I teach.

POWER PLAYING IMPROVISATIONS

Some of the most successful improvisations I have seen done are based on power playing. Power playing is a fact of life. If you think of the intentions of all humanity as a gravitation toward the pole of wanting to destroy a relationship and the pole of wanting to create a relationship, you have begun to tap the energy source of power playing. Power playing has a fascinating dramatic strength.

Famous Plays with Power Playing Relationships

There are good examples of power playing relationships in every period, form, and mode of theatre. For instance:

Creon vs Oedipus in Sophocles' *Oedipus Rex* or Antigone vs. Creon in his *Antigone.*

Peniculus vs. Menaechmus in Plautus' *The Menaechmi.*

Richard vs. Anne in Shakespere's *Richard III* or Beatrice vs. Benedict in his *Much Ado About Nothing* or Katherine vs. Petruchio in his *The Taming of the Shrew.*

Lydia vs. Mrs. Malaprop in Sheridan's *The Rivals.*

Torvald vs. his wife, Nora, in Ibsen's *A Doll's House.*

Blanche vs. Stanley in Tennessee Williams' *A Streetcar Named Desire.*

And almost anybody vs. anybody in the more contemporary plays of Harold Pinter, Eugene Ionesco, Edward Albee, Sam Shepherd, Christopher Durang, Athol Fugard and Carol Churchyll.

To Need, Not to Want

When you set up power playing improvisations, you should make the stakes as high as possible.

If each actor plays the strength of his intentions and does his best to overcome the obstacles presented by his opponent, then the improvisation has the best chance of coming alive. Don't *want* to create or destroy; *need* to create or destroy.

Two people trying to create a love relationship with each other is not a power play; it is a love scene. Two men or two women trying to destroy each other can make an exciting improvisation but it can also quickly turn into a physical fight if it isn't assumed by both players, even though the assumption may be make-believe, that one player is a good deal bigger and stronger than the other player.

If a power playing improvisation begins to show signs of physical violence, I warn both players to back off. If the threat of violence continues, I stop the improvisation. Pick a member of your group to act as referee.

Remember Your 4 W's

Remember you can't play an intention or follow an inner monologue in a vacuum. Have the referee whisper the intention to be used in the ear of each of the opponents. Intentions are to be kept a secret until the power play is over. When each of the opponents knows what intention he will play, but before the power play begins, the opponents must get together as actors, not opponents, and prepare a framework for the improvisation. They must give the improvisation a specific place and time.

As you would in doing any ensemble improvisation, give your characters a specific relationship and each character a specific profession. At least one of the players should come into the place where the power play will occur from a specific place where something specific was going on.

When the power play begins, use activities and create basic obstacles to each activity. Let an inner monologue develop and use extrasensory physicalization. Keep yourself physically and sensorially alive and try to use activity to get what you need to get from your opponent. Use words but don't depend on them. If your opponent isn't attractive enough or unattractive enough for your purposes, substitute a personalization for him.

A List of Tactics

For those of you who are not conscious of having participated, at least once or twice, in real life power plays, here are some fundamental tactics to use in power playing improvisations:

To Destroy a Relationship:	*To Create a Love or Friendship Relationship:*
Use the aggressive, negative approach	*Use the positive, supportive approach*
Attack with harsh invective and/or vocal power	*Retreat with praise or verbal gentleness*
Intimidate or threaten physically	*Physically retire or relax and stand your ground*
Leave or turn your back	*Come forward with open arms*
Give the silent treatment	*Sooth physically or vocally*
Answer passion or emotion with cold logic	*Calmly express your feelings*
Treat as a child	*Treat as a hero or heroine*

Order around	*Wait upon*
Pretend indifference	*Express understanding*

Pairs, Not Groups

I find very little value in power playing improvisations that pit a group versus a group or a group versus an individual. They usually end in chaos. Man versus woman of course will work as well if not better than man versus man or woman versus woman. Child versus adult can have extraordinary results.

Rules and Strategy

The most important rule is that each player must play to win. You must keep putting obstacles in the way of what you think your opponent is trying to do to you. You must keep trying to fulfill your inention, to get what you need. You can't give up until the referee says, "Stop!" Winning is getting what you need. There may be no winner but that doesn't mean the improvisation has been unsuccessful. It can mean quite the opposite — that both actors have learned to survive in a power playing situation. As long as both players are alive and kicking, I urge the players to keep going.

The second most important rule is that you can pretend to need the opposite of what you actually need. You must constantly maintain your given intention. Nevertheless, if your opponent isn't sure what your given intention is, he won't know when you are trying to get what you need by direct methods and when you are pretending to try to get the opposite of what you need. If you want to destroy a bad relationship and destructive tactics are getting you nowhere, you can change tactics suddenly and pretend you need to create a good relationship. You may confuse your opponent enough to get the advantage over him. As soon as you get your opponent confused or off guard, the climax of the power play may be near. You can change back to your original destructive tactics and give your opponent the coup de grace.

If you need to create a love or friendship relationship and you suddenly pretend to need to destroy that relationship, your opponent may very well back off and forget, for the moment, his need to destroy. Then, press the point home. Give your opponent a big hug and the game is over.

You may leave the place of competition with the intention of staying away or under the pretense of leaving for good. The other player will deal with your leaving as either a fulfillment of his intention or an obstacle to that intention. If you leave the place of competition, however, and the referee says, "Keep playing!" you must find a way to get back in. As soon as you leave the place, of course, you immediately run the risk of losing. It may not have seemed so, but your opponent's intention may have been to get rid of you.

Lessons to Be Learned

These improvisations obviously teach you that meanness and cunning are just as likely to win in this game of life as are charm and honesty. Don't you want to play some of the great villains or villainesses in theatre as well as the great heroes or heroines? If you have already played the lover, try another power play and play the destroyer.

Another important lesson to be learned doing these improvisations is to not rely solely on words. Physical relationship, activity and behavior may work better than words. Standing over someone to theaten him can intimidate that person, but cowering beneath your opponent and calmly saying, "Go ahead and hurt me. You're too strong for me. I can't fight back," is an attitude that can be just as unsettling. You may not stop a psychotic killer by displaying your helplessness but most normal people will think twice before hurting someone verbally or physically who seems helpless to resist their attack.

Power playing offers an infinite variation on the same theme. Doing these improvisations forces the actor to be aware of what is happening at all times. It teaches him to think and react quickly and to work moment to moment.

BEATS AND TRANSITIONS

An actor mustn't think as a director does in tempos and rhythms of action or he will become result-oriented, but an actor can be aware of when one beat ends and another beat begins. Power playing improvisations dramatically illustrate beat changes.

A change of beat is when one action ends and another one begins. When you are trying to fulfill an intention and you stop trying, or you are using a specific tactic to get what you want and you change your tactic, that is a change of beat.

If I'm trying to destroy you and I suddenly start to love you, the beat has changed. If I want you to come with me into the bedroom and you stop resisting and come with me, the beat has changed. If I have tried to persuade you to be loving and not hateful, and I begin to pretend that I dislike you as much as you seem to dislike me, a beat has changed.

As the beat changes there is usually a moment of transition.

The trick is to take the time to let the transition happen before you start to play the next beat. If a mother has been trying to get a child to behave and the child stops misbehaving, the mother needs a moment to gather herself. She needs a moment to decide to give the child a hug.

Scoring Beats and Transitions to Text

When you begin to put actors' work to a playwright's text or a screenwriter's screenplay, you will see the value in scoring transitions and beats. For instance, a passage of dialogue will be useful in trying to hurt someone but a transition will occur (the person you tried to hurt *is* hurt and begins to cry). The next passage will be useful for your apologizing and trying to stop the flow of tears.

To remind yourself to use the two passages according to plan, you simply write in the margin of your script, alongside the appropriate passage, "Hurt" and "Mend." Don't forget, however, to also mark the transition. Give yourself a chance to realize whether he is crying.

Moment-to-Moment Work in Rehearsal and Performance

One of the useful lessons power playing improvisations teaches is the ability to work with what happens, not with what you anticipate will happen.

Anticipation

Yes, in performance the moment-to-moment work done in rehearsal has to be repeated but the secret is to not anticipate. If you are playing an intention in a performance or a scene class and you know, because it was set that way in rehearsal, that eventually you are not going to get what you want the way you are trying to get it, forget that a transition is coming. Play your intention to the fullest as if nothing were going to happen to change your tactics.

Stay with your intention. Deal with each obstacle you encounter. You will be playing moment to moment despite the fact that in the back of your mind you know what is coming. If you play each moment for what it is, the next moment will be upon you before you know it. Concentrate on what's happening, not what is going to happen.

Don't kiss someone knowing he or she is going to push you away. Kiss him or her to get the full taste of his or her lips. When you get pushed away, you will have a dramatic moment to deal with — not a moment without transition that passed you by, that never happened.

There are actors' exercises you will do that will help you extend your ability to create a character but, except for exercises in emotional release, you have now practiced every level of actors' work and every form of improvisation that can help you prepare a role in a playwright's script. You are ready for a scene class.

The director may tell you what your character wants, but why put yourself in a position in which you are subject to the dictation of terms? Learn in scene classes to make your own decision about who your character is. (Davies High School, Lincoln, Rhode Island; photo by Lawrence Sasso, The Observer, Greenville, Rhode Island.)

6. How to Work a Script

Read the Whole Script

When you begin to work on a scene, don't neglect the processes you have practiced. Before you begin to work on a scene from a script, you must read the whole script. You must decide what your character's intention is at that moment in your character's life. You can't make an arbitrary decision as you did when you were doing improvisations to practice the process of creating a character. When you are building a role in a playwright's script, nobody is going to whisper your charcter's intention in your ear. Eventually, when you are building a role in a production of a play or a movie, the director may tell you what your character wants, but why put yourself in a position in which you are subject to the dictation of terms? Learn in scene classes to make your own decision about who your character is and what he wants.

Your character's intention in a scene is dependent on what he wants out of life and what he wants out of the situation in which he finds himself during the entire time span of the script. A scene takes place during only part of that time span.

Don't Play Ideas or States of Being

Reading the play and doing research will give you ideas about who your character is but, as you already know, playing abstract ideas, descriptive adjectives, or states of being can get you in trouble. Put the thoughts you have about your character in the back of your mind and let them have a subconscious effect on your work. Consciously put to use the actors' work you have practiced to create a multidimensional human character.

Research

Do research on people whose lives and times are similar to your character's life and times. Create a past life for your character and make your sense-memories his sense-memories.

Improvise

Find out who your character is by doing improvisations that allow you to live your character's life outside the confines of his life in the script. Do ensemble improvisations that allow you to relate to the other characters in the script, especially the character or characters in the scene. Relate to the people in your character's life in habitual situations, situations that would have taken place before the time span of the script. Do power playing improvisations with characters with whom your character has power playing relationships.

Establish your character's profession. Do an improvisation in his work place. Put on clothes he would have on at the time the scene takes place. Create your character's physical age by physicalizing his specific physical states of being. As you improvise, do what your character wants to do. Allow your character to physically behave and think and feel. Trust in the fact that, without your being conscious of it, your character's physical mannerisms, mental attitudes and emotional feelings will evolve by themselves.

APPROACHING A SCENE

If the place where the scene takes place is a place where your character has spent and is spending a good deal of his time, do a 4 W's solo improvisation in that place. Discover what's there. Know every aspect of that place, 360 degrees around you.

Also, very importantly, create a geography for your character outside of where the scene takes place. Realize in the space between you and the audience, the direction toward which you, as your character, go to work, the direction toward where you want to go on vacation. Know the specific direction toward any place to which you refer with the playwright's words. Vary the directions toward specific places so that you can focus your sense-memory imagination of each place in a different direction than any other place.

As you move in the space in which the scene takes place, let yourself physically relate to the places outside of the space. Move toward them or away from them. As you verbally refer to them, let yourself gesture toward them. Don't, however, feel compelled to gesture toward a place every time you refer to that place. Let gestures happen as they will.

Put the place far enough away from the space where the scene takes place for your facial expressions, which will reflect your feelings about that place, to carry across to the audience. If the place is indoors and you put imaginary windows and mirrors in the space between you and the audience, they will help you focus or project your thoughts, sense-memories and feelings toward a specific place outside.

If the place where the scene takes place is new to your character, make his discovery of that place part of the initial work in that place. Discovering the place may very well be an important part of your character's intention. If the playwright tells you that the scene takes place on a summer evening at six o'clock, you still must decide what sort of a summer evening it is. Is it hot and humid or cool and crisp?

Work the Scene as if You were Improvising and Develop a Pattern of What Is Happening

Finally, you are ready to do your first stage of work on the scene itself. Work with your partner or partners as if you were doing an ensemble improvisation. Don't improvise the playwright's words from a general concept of those words. Work with the script in your hand or close at hand and put the playwright's words to use.

As if you were improvising, don't plan what is going to happen. Find activity to fulfill intention. Deal with obstacles that arise. Be aware of and relate to the other character or characters. Let your intentions and feelings about other characters move you physically toward them or away from them. Connect to the time of day, the weather, and your specific physical states of being, including age. Realize what is pleasant or unpleasant. Let an inner monologue develop.

Put the Playwright's Words to Use

As you work, use the playwright's words to help you do what your character is doing. If the words don't connect to what your character is doing, find out what your character could be doing that would make the playwright's words more useful. When the pattern of the playwright's words fits the pattern of the actor's work you are going to bring your character and the situation alive, the first stage of work is over.

MEMORIZING WORDS

Don't sit down and commit the playwright's words to memory. If you memorize this way, when your character speaks, he will sound as if he had memorized the words he is speaking. Learn your words by walking the scene and connecting your character's words to what he is doing when he is using those words.

Your character's words shouldn't only be connected to physical activity. He might very well be connecting them to a sense-memory or an inner monologue. He may be physically inactive for the moment. Words will come alive as human expression as long as they are connected to a specific level of human existence. They may be connected to a number of levels at the same time.

Score Your Script Before You Are Blocked into a Scene by a Director

Don't ever memorize your words before they are connected to the moment-to-moment life you have created for your character. Score actors' work in the margins of your script. Actors' work should always support and give life to a playwright's words.

As a second stage of your work on a scene, rehearse the scene as if you hadn't decided what was going to happen moment to moment. Use the playwright's words. Fulfill each moment and learn not to anticipate. Be willing to adapt your work to the work your partner or partners are doing. Don't set a pattern of actors' work that has to be followed no matter what. Let the pattern evolve.

As the final step, score the scene with beats of action and the transitions between those beats.

Obviously, after you have done all this work you will have blocked your own scene. When an entire script is being rehearsed while working toward a performance, most directors will block the script scene by scene. When you are rehearsing an entire script, try to do the work you did to prepare a scene for a scene class before the director blocks and directs you into a scene. If the pattern of the work you have done disagrees with the pattern the director gives you, you will be in a position to suggest alternatives to his plan. You may not get them, but you will deserve the respect a responsible, prepared actor should expect to have.

If you let yourself believe in the entire dramatic event you will release emotion spontaneously. (Left to right: Buddy Rogers, Robert Curtis, Gloria Swanson, author Carlton Colyer and Betty Rollin in pre-Broadway tour of Red Letter Day *by Andrew Rosenthal.)*

7. RELEASING EMOTION

AVAILABILITY

Availability is the actor's magic word. Being available is the ultimate state of being for an actor to attain. Being available means being relaxed and concentrated enough to allow yourself, in character, on stage or in front of a camera, to behave and express yourself with the multidimensionality and truth of a human being.

If you made yourself available to the work in the preceding exercises and improvisations you have allowed your voice, your body and your face to express themselves. You have made yourself available to relationships with your fellow actors in ensemble improvisations.

Now is the time to make yourself available to release your or your character's emotions. You may have thought, when you began the study of acting, that laughing and crying on cue and in character was one of the first things an actor learned. Because, however, multidimensional human expression of emotion on stage or in front of a camera is dependent on your choice of one or more of the many elements of actors' work, you needed first to have practiced all of the elements of that work. Therefore, I have saved the release of emotion until now.

As you practiced your actors' work, you must have been aware that feelings began to surface when you found the essence of a pleasant or unpleasant sense-memory, when you created obstacles to activities, when you created specific pleasant and unpleasant physical states of being and when you played a powerful intention or an inner monologue and were either frustrated by not getting what you wanted or were rewarded by getting what you wanted.

Human feelings began to rise in you because these are the situations that build emotions in human beings. They are actors' work situations that are the equivalent of actual life situations.

You have already expressed emotions with vocal inflection, facial expression and physical gesture. You may have laughed, cried or exploded with anger or elation in the midst of concentrating on actors' work that didn't necessarily call for laughter, tears or a burst of anger or elation.

When you are auditioning, rehearsing and performing and you are in character and involved in a moment-to-moment dramatic situation, strong feelings will rise up in you as they did when you were practicing your actors' work. You will release those emotions if and when you are prepared to release them.

The Release of Human Emotion in the Public World

Now that you can create a character, you must take that character and ask him to live in a theatrical world as if he was living in the actual world. You must persuade yourself, as that character, to release emotion in front of a camera or an audience, in auditions, rehearsals and performances.

Many inexperienced actors are too shy to do this. Because of social conditioning some actors can't permit themselves to release emotion in public. Other actors can cry in public but they can't laugh or vice versa.

Some actors release emotion easily in the public world of theatre and movies. However, the emotions they express — their tears, laughter and outbursts of anger or elation — are always the same no matter what the situation or the character they are playing. Their emotional expression is too general. It has not been connected to the human multidimensionality of specific actors' work. In all these cases there are lessons to learn and there is work to be done.

A Good Actor Is a Good Listener

It is said that a good actor is a good listener. Like all adages there is some truth in this. It doesn't mean that, if your character doesn't want to listen to what the other character or characters are saying and you stop listening, you are a bad actor. It does mean that you should stay in character and be aware not only of what you are doing but also of what the other character or characters are doing, aware of what is going on inside of you and, yes, aware of audience response.

If moment to moment you are aware of what is happening on all these levels, if you let yourself believe in the entire dramatic event, when something happens to spark emotion in your character, if you are relaxed and concentrated, you will more than likely release that emotion spontaneously.

The problem is that many actors don't relax and concentrate at a moment of emotional release. As their characters they stop concentrating on the dramatic situation. They become aware as actors that they are about to burst with emotion in public. They become tense and they shut off the emotional release.

The Secret of Availability to Emotional Release

When you are ready to laugh or cry or explode with anger or elation, if the rising of emotion produces tension, don't argue with yourself about whether it's actors' tension or your character's tension. Tension chokes up or chokes off any human being's release of emotion. Don't try to force yourself to cry or laugh. All you will get for your pains is more tension.

To release emotion you must relax and concentrate on the dramatic moment or on your actor's work as thoroughly as possible. If you or your character becomes tense, stay in character but do a quick relaxation exercise. Stand or sit in alignment, gently move your head with the neck's seven vertebrae, take a deep breath with your bellows and let the laughter or tears or anger or elation ride out of you on what could be a sigh but could also be the words your character is speaking. If your character is speaking at the time of the release of emotion, don't stop speaking. You and your character can laugh, cry, explode with anger or elation and talk at the same time.

Vulnerability

There is a thin line between availability and vulnerability but I think the line is definable. You are emotionally vulnerable when your actor's feelings are at stake. You are emotionally available when you are willing to substitute your emotions for your character's emotions.

When Vivian Nathan stopped rehearsal and told me I couldn't talk to her as I had, I became vulnerable. I was the insecure actor worrying about his job. After we had talked and had become acquainted and I had relaxed, knowing my actor's ego was no longer at stake, I was able to make myself available to the mother and son relationship. I was ready to feel as Jamie would feel.

The Audience

In live theatre the audience is there. They are part of the event. If you try to shut them out entirely you will lose in the attempt. Your inner monologue will be out of character. You will begin to hear yourself saying to yourself such things as: "I wish they would go away." "I hope they like me." "Why are they so quiet?" "I don't dare look at them."

If you remain connected to what your character and the other characters are doing, audience response, just like vocal and facial expression, will take care of itself. Applause, gasps, silence — any audience expression of emotion — will only reinforce what you are doing.

The audience is a participant in the dramatic event. They will identify with the characters with whom they sympathize and they will be alienated by the characters with whom they are not in sympathy. If you are the hero or the heroine and you begin to cry, wouldn't the audience's tears encourage you to cry even more? If you are playing the villain and you begin to laugh at something evil and the audience reacts with anger, wouldn't that anger support and encourage your laughter?

Whether their emotional response is in support of your character or in opposition to your character, you should be encouraged by their response. If you and your character are connected to the dramatic event, the audience will react to your character, not to the actor playing the character. Their anger, laughter, tears or elation will support your release of emotion, not interrupt it.

By the way, you should stay in character; don't stop crying or laughing if that's what you are doing, but take a pause in the dramatic action until audience response begins to subside. Then you won't be interrupting their involvement in the dramatic situation any more than you allowed them to interrupt your involvement in the same situation.

PREPARATION

There are times when you can't allow emotional release to happen moment to moment; you have to prepare for it. Emotional release often has to happen on cue because you and the playwright and the director want it that way.

What if a moment in the dramatic event affects you emotionally but only to the degree that your feelings surface as vocal inflection and facial and physical expression but not the laughter or tears or burst of anger or elation you want at that moment?

What if you are offstage or off camera, not involved in the dramatic events on stage or on camera, and you have to enter laughing, crying or bursting with anger or elation?

In both cases you are going to have to prepare, you are going to have to create your own dramatic moment. You are going to have to concentrate on something that is funny enough or sad enough or annoying enough or happy enough to work for you.

You already know the actors' work that stirs emotions:

>*The essense of pleasant or unpleasant sense-memory or the physicalization of that memory;*

>*A specific pleasant or unpleasant physical state of being;*

>*An obstacle to an activity;*

>*A strong intention or inner monologue that angers you when you can't get what you want or pleases you when you do get what you want.*

Releasing Emotion on Cue

In rehearsal, when you are working out the pattern of actors' work that will fit the pattern of the playwright's words, what you do is score in actors' work you know will stir up the emotion you want to release. You score in that work far enough in advance of the cue so that the emotion will build to the point where you can't hold it in any longer; you have to release it when the cue comes.

When you have prepared emotional release as part of the dramatic pattern in rehearsal, you need not anticipate the moment of emotional release as you are performing. If you relax and concentrate thoroughly on the work you have given yourself to stir up the emotion, when the cue comes, the emotional release will take care of itself.

Examples of Releasing Emotion on Cue

When I was working on Jamie's last scene in *Long Day's Journey Into Night,* I decided that I wanted Jamie to cry as he said, "Christ, I'd never dreamed before that any women but whores took dope!" I found a sense-memory of my own that related closely to what Jamie would be remembering. My sense-memory made me want to cry and, strangely enough, to laugh.

As I scored my sense-memory into the pattern of my actors' work, I decided to begin concentrating on my image a number of moments before I said the words that would cue the emotional release. O'Neill's words that I spoke that led up to the cue seemed to want to drag the tears and laughter out of me. I held them in, however, until I got to, "Christ, I'd . . . ." By the time I got to, ". . . whores took dope!" I was crying and laughing and talking all at the same time. Of course, the fact that I had convinced myself that Jamie was dead drunk helped me give myself permission to release any emotion I felt like releasing.

I played Jake Latta in Tennessee Williams' *The Night of the*

Iguana. Jake is a tour bus director. He has been sent by his company to replace Shannon, the leading character in the play, who has been misdirecting a bus tour of tropical Mexico. Jake is fat and, to find Shannon in a strange hotel above the sea, he has to climb a steep hill in the humid heat. Shannon is a romantic-alcoholic and he has long-winded explanations and excuses for his peculiar behavior as a tour director. Despite the heat, Shannon's babbling, and a struggle with Shannon to get the bus key away from him, Jake has stayed cool, calm and collected but at the end of the scene I wanted Jake, out of nowhere, to burst with anger and leave.

Just before he leaves, however, Jake has to stand and listen to one more long story from Shannon. I had already physicalized sweat and mopped it off my face with a huge handkerchief. Now, as I stood listening, the sweat began to trickle down my back and between the cheeks of my behind. Then a mosquito bit the back of my neck. Shannon droned on. The sweat dripped. The bite itched. I heard Shannon's last words. My lines, "Go on, lie back in your hammock; that's all you're good for, Shannon" came out of me like the growl from a grizzly bear. I left the hotel and Shannon in silence for once in his life.

The growl of anger was frightening because it seemed to come from nowhere. It had come, however, from my building the intensity of Jake's discomfort with the sweat and mosquitoes I had physicalized for him.

EXERCISES TO ALLOW YOURSELF EMOTIONAL RELEASE

If you have tried giving yourself moment to moment to a dramatic situation that should build emotion to the point where it releases itself and the laughter, tears, or bursts of anger or elation didn't happen, then you need to do some actors' exercises to persuade you to allow yourself to release emotion in public.

Gibberish

No matter how much they relax and concentrate and prepare, some actors still resist expressing emotion in public. There are three exercises that can help lower that resistance.

In your repertory of experiences, find one that is packed with emotion. The emotions don't have to be negative: anger, depression, etc. They can be positive: joy, elation, etc. It is sometimes more difficult to laugh on stage than it is to cry.

Once you have found a story about a true experience that has a lot of emotional impact, get up in front of a group of your

fellow actors and tell the story in gibberish. Don't leave out any
details. You are speaking gibberish; your audience won't know
exactly what you are talking about but make them try to understand.
Try to reveal your very personal feelings.

Begin at the beginning and take your time. Connect to the
sense-memories and try hard to convey your feelings about those
memories. Let the gibberish flow. The fact that you can't use words
will frustrate you. If your frustration makes you tense, relax. Use
more of a variety of sounds in your gibberish. Use your hands, arms
and body to express yourself. Keep relaxed and concentrated but
struggle to make yourself convey to your listeners what was pleasant
or unpleasant about what happened.

When emotion begins to surface, keep telling the story in
gibberish. Repeat your description of what happened and is happening now to make you feel strongly. Share your very personal feelings.
If you begin to laugh or to cry or to hear anger or elation in the
sounds of your gibberish, go ahead! Laugh or cry or whatever to
your heart's content, but try to keep your story going and to repeat
what you feel strongly about. Whether you just express emotion
or the emotion releases and bursts out of you, you have become
available in public to your own private feelings. If you released
emotion and kept struggling to express what you were feeling with
gibberish, don't be ashamed of yourself for having let your emotions
go while talking a kind of baby talk. Be thrilled. Your actor's instrument is tuned to the point where you are an available person and
an expressive actor.

The Extended Vowel Sound Song

If the gibberish exercises didn't work for you try this:
Warm up your voice.
Relax physically and mentally.
Pick a simple song you know well.
Stand in alignment in front of your fellow actors.
Use your bellows.
Sing each vowel sound of your song but extend the sound
as long as you can on one breath. (You can sing the consonant
sounds but extend only the vowel sounds.)

It doesn't matter if you sing well or stay in tune; just keep
relaxed and breathe fully and deeply with your bellows.

Let the vowel sounds ride out of the center of you, the guts
of you.

Make eye-to-eye contact with individual listeners.

Keep the vowel sounds coming. Repeat the song if you have
to over and over again. Extend each sound as long as you can on
one breath.

If emotional expression comes into your voice or you can feel emotion welling up in you, let it ride out on the extended vowel sounds. Let sound carry emotion out of you to your audience.

If the emotion you begin to release is unexpected, don't deny it; let it flow out with vowel sound.

Don't stop extending sound after sound to cry, to laugh or burst with anger or elation. Release emotion and sound at the same time.

When you feel emotionally spent, stop the exercise.

If Gibberish or The Extended Vowel Song Sound didn't work for you, there is another effective exercise.

Private Moment

This exercise is recommended for adults only. It is not recommended for teen-agers in the throes of self-consciousness and growing up.

The exercise is a Lee Strasberg creation designed for a very shy woman member of the Actors Studio. She had a fine actor's instrument but she couldn't let go emotionally in public. Even when emotion wasn't involved, her vocal and physical expression was inhibited. Lee asked her to do something in front of us that, if she did it in private, she would stop doing it if someone came upon her doing it. We all immediately wondered if he meant a sexual or bathroom activity. "Not necessarily," he said. Lee was never one to give easy answers to direct questions.

Because the exercise worked for the woman in question, many of us tried it. I have seen some private moments that did involve sexual or bathroom acivities. One or two involved nudity but that was when performing in the nude à la Living Theatre was the rage. I have, however, seen many private moments after my time at the Actors Studio and none of them involved nudity, or bathroom or explicit sexual acts.

Many of the private moments I have witnessed have been successful. The actor may not have fully released emotion during the exercise but often physical expression and, where applicable, vocal expression was enhanced as the actor progressed further and further into the moment. More important was the effect of the exercise on the work the actor did after the private moment. The exercise gave the actor permission to express publicly what until then had been in his private domain.

The Private Moment Exercise is much like the Solo 4 W's Improvisation in that the actor sets up a space he knows well and involves himself in activities and sense-memories. Unlike the Solo 4 W's Improvisation, however, he ultimately involves himself in an activity he has previously only done in private, something up until

now he would have stopped doing if anyone came upon him doing
it.

Real Objects

It helps to bring actual, personal objects to relate to while
doing the exercise. In fact, by the time you are ready to do this
exercise, you are ready to bring real objects to all of your work.
Having worked for some time with physicalized objects, you will
appreciate that everything, especially personal things, have a life
of their own. Real objects will now come alive for you, especially
when you involve them in an activity or use them to focus an inner
sense-memory or as part of your concentration on an inner
monologue. Remember total awareness involves all the senses as
well as all the levels of actors' work. If one sense-memory or level
of work doesn't bring you alive and help you concentrate, then
another sense-memory or level of work will.

The objects I have seen that become most useful to a private
moment are: letters, yearbooks, photographs, records and tapes,
stuffed animals, or any momento of a poignant moment in the
actor's past.

Examples of Private Moments

Some kinds of private moments that were useful in releasing
inhibition were:

Dancing to provocative music;

Singing in the shower or tub (The water was physicalized —
I have seen actors work both in clothes and nude. For some actors
behaving as if nude was enough to release inhibition.);

Reading a private letter aloud;

Picking your nose or removing blackheads;

Exploring your body while looking at yourself in a mirror
(either nude or as if nude);

Practicing a song, a dance, an instrument, or a speech the
actor doesn't know well;

Rehearsing what you are going to say to tell someone off or
to get someone to love you;

Going about everyday business while having intense sense-
memories of someone to whom you are physically very attracted;

Going about everyday business while listening to music you
associate closely with someone to whom you are physically very
attracted;

Moving voluptuously to music.

Those are some of the exercises I can remember. The idea, of
course, it not to copy somebody else's exercise. Use one of my ex-

amples if that is something you have done in private and you honestly feel doing it in public would help you release inhibition. If you don't find a good choice for you among my examples then find your own private moment, but before you make a choice, see yourself doing it in the past and then imagine someone, even family or lovers, coming into your space while you were doing it. If you wouldn't have stopped doing what you were doing, you don't have a true private moment to use. Keep thinking.

Some people literally have no inhibitions. If you aren't inhibited emotionally, physically or vocally, then there is no reason you have to do the exercise.

Welcome to the world of actors' availability. If you dared to do a Private Moment you probably will never have to dare yourself again to make your private self available in public, in front of an audience or a camera.

Affective Memory and Emotional Recall

According to Webster's Dictionary an affective memory is a memory that has an "emotional influence." In actors' terms, an affective memory is a sense-memory that evokes or recalls a specific emotional release, an emotional release you had in a situation in actual life that is similar to the dramatic situation you are working on. The dramatic situation developed out of the script, however, doesn't evoke the emotional release you want.

In this case, you need to do an affective memory exercise. Doing this exercise will not only recreate the emotional release you want, but more importantly, it will also recall the exact sensory experience that triggered that release.

You can score the sensory experience that triggers the emotional release where you want it in the dramatic situation in your script. You will not only cry on cue, you will also cry the exact kind of tears you want to cry or should be crying.

I only do affective memory exercises with adult students who have had as much actors' training as you have had.

I forbid my students to use what was a traumatic experience as an affective memory. If an experience was psychologically damaging in the past, it will be psychologically damaging again if you repeat it. Actors' training is not psychoanalysis.

I have done hundreds of affective memory exercises with my students and at least ninety per cent of them have been successful. The students were practiced in extrasensory concentration. They had overcome their inhibitions about expressing emotion in public. They could relax and concentrate thoroughly and allow themselves to become available to their feelings.

Many actors can do affective memory exercises on their own

but you may need someone to coach you through your first one, especially if you expect someone to hold your hand after you are emotionally spent.

If you don't get the results you predicted you would get, try again another day with another affective memory. The emotional release that happens in your first choice of a sense-memory experience may, however, be more honest and multidimensional than the emotional release you had hoped for. You may laugh and get angry all at once. It could be that the unpredicted emotional release is a better choice for the dramatic moment in the script than the predicated emotional release would have been.

The Affective Memory Exercise

Make a choice. Pick a specific emotionally charged event to recall.

Do a physical warm-up exercise.

Sit in a straight-backed chair in alignment.

Close your eyes and relax both physically and mentally.

Just as you did when you took a sense-memory trip to the pleasant, outdoor place or the childhood play place, take your time.

Start at the beginning of the day in question and with your eyes closed and maintaining alignment and physical relaxation, find your way step by step, moment by moment through that day toward the emotionally charged moment. If the event happened early in the morning, start the evening before.

Work extrasensorially. Don't only see things and people. Listen, touch, smell and taste. If you want to reach out and physicalize a specific object, do it. Keep your eyes shut, however, and maintain alignment and relaxation.

Experience again every little thing, event and person as the day progresses. Feel the warmth or the cold of the day. Feel the texture and weight of the clothes you have on. Open doors and windows if that's what you did that day. Prepare and taste the food you had for each meal. Listen to the sounds around you.

Travel from one place to another if that is what you did but remember your travels.

As you get closer and closer to the emotional experience, take even more time. Let your senses remember every detail.

As you begin to get excited because the event is about to take place, relax physically. Let yourself breathe but stay connected to the event.

When you begin to cry, laugh or explode with anger or elation, relax that much more. Stay connected to what is happening. Don't force the emotional release, just let it happen. Release! Let it all out! Open your eyes and laugh, cry, bellow with anger or howl with elation. If there are words involved in the expression and release of the emotion, let yourself speak. Later you can substitute the playwright's words for your words.

The Trigger

When you have come down from the emotional experience of the affective memory, let yourself remember the essence of the sense-memory experience that triggered the laughter, tears, anger or elation. Close your eyes, relax and reconnect to the sensory experience a few moments before the emotional release.

The sensory trigger to the emotional release may be the last thing you expected it to be: a door slamming, a word said, a dog barking, a Venetian blind going up or down. Whatever it was, remember which of your senses gave you the strongest memory of that trigger.

As you reconnect with the essence of the experience you probably will begin to cry, laugh or explode with anger or elation again. That's good. Now you have the exact sensory experience that will trigger a specific emotional release.

Remember the work from the script before and after the cue on which you want to release emotion. Open your eyes. Remember what you and your character are doing when you say the words. Do what you and your character are doing and say out loud what your character is supposed to say. Begin an inner sense-memory of the affective memory experience. Start the inner sense-memory a couple of moments before the emotional trigger. Speak, do, remember at the same time. Let the emotional release happen when it will. Let the words you are speaking and the dramatic experience you are having help the emotion to surface. If the emotional release comes too quickly or too late, readjust the place in the script or the moment in the sequence of what your character is doing where you begin to concentrate on the affective memory.

When you want the emotional release to cease, stay in character but disconnect with a sense-memory or physicalization of some favorite indulgence totally unrelated to the affective memory experience.

Now, just because your entire physical, mental sensory and emotional instrument has been tuned doesn't mean that it will stay in tune.

Continue to do your physical and vocal warm-ups. Use your relaxation exercises.

When you get cobwebs in your sense-memory process — when any of your basic actor's work gets sand in its works — return to the basic exercises and improvisations and get rid of the cobwebs and the sand.

Next, let's put the tuned instrument to use in scene classes, auditions, rehearsals and performances.

Stay connected to what is happening. Don't force the emotional release, just let is happen. Release! Let it all out! (Author Carlton Colyer as Tom with Betty Field as Amanda in The Glass Menagerie, *by Tennessee Williams, Boston, Massachusetts.)*

II. PUTTING TECHNIQUE TO USE

The auditioner wants to see how your body, unencumbered with objects and activity, works to bring a character alive. (Author Carlton Colyer, Dwight Englewood School, Englewood, New Jersey.)

1. SCENE CLASSES

Now that you have done all that is required to build a technique and have carefully tuned your actor's instrument, the next step is equally difficult and demanding. Putting actors' work to a challenging playwright's or screenwriter's script is not a simple matter. It takes endless practice. I don't want to discourage you but, once again, you must work step by step. Much of what you must do, however, is as much fun as it is work. You will be practicing the technique you will use for the rest of your acting career. You will be doing the work you must do to become a fine, professional actor.

You must learn to create a variety of multidimensional characters. You must learn to build roles in a number of kinds of plays. A good first step is to join a scene class.

You should work in that scene class for at least a year before you play a role in a production. Don't be tempted to play roles in high school, college, university, or any amateur productions until you are confident that you can put actors' work to a variety of period styles and dramatic forms.

My further advice is to continue to work, if possible, in advanced scene classes for still another year before attempting to audition for a part in a professional production. Good actors keep attending scene classes throughout their careers.

There are three main sources of scene classes in the United States: universities and colleges, regional theatre conservatories and private studios. Most colleges and universities now have theatre departments. Some of the private liberal arts colleges and universities that have the highest reputations for their undergraduate schools have good theatre departments. Some don't. The same thing is true about state universities. The nice thing about state universities is that they are much less expensive than the private schools. There are always scholarships and financial aid programs, however, that can make private universities and colleges available to students who can't afford the $80,000 it can cost for four years at a private institution. In any case, it is possible to get a good undergraduate, all-around, liberal arts education and to be well trained as an actor at the same time.

AUDITION MONOLOGUES

Theatre departments in colleges and universities, regional theatre conservatories, and some private studios will ask you to prepare two monologues with which to audition for acceptance into their training programs. A monologue is a long speech given by a character within the dramatic event of a script. The character making the long speech may be talking to himself but more than likely is talking to another character or group of characters. In many monologues the character is telling some sort of a story.

If you are applying for entrance into an undergraduate program or any scene class for beginners, you usually have not practiced the techniques of applying actors' work to a playwright's text, but you must do the best you can. The people who will be auditioning you will not expect you to be an accomplished actor. They are looking for the potential you have for further training as an actor. You now have all the technique needed to score actors' work to a playwright's text. I have given you the basics for putting that technique to work. You may be able to find a good teacher of acting in a private studio or a high school drama coach who believes in the creation of multidimensional human characters to help you. I teach in a private studio and I recently helped a young man to prepare for his audition for New York University. He passed his audition and he got an early acceptance into the university and its prestigious theatre department.

Beginning Audition Monologues for Scene Classes

Start right now to read twentieth-century plays that take place in the twentieth century. They are listed under Dramatic Forms in the Building Roles section of this book. Read plays from the Comedy or Tragicomedy lists. Read plays you have already read in an English class. This time, read them as an acting student, not a student of English. Read plays you know you should read because they are famous. Find a long speech or a number of fairly long speeches you can put together as a monologue. If the fairly long speeches are interrupted by another character's responses, cut the responses. The monologue you use should be spoken by a character with whom you identify because that character's personality and life experience may be similar to your own. Don't pick monologues that require an accent. Don't pick overly dramatic speeches that ask you to burst with emotion. Nobody should expect you to do that as yet. Don't use monologues from the classics or Shakespeare or plays that take place before the twentieth century.

106

Two Two-and-a-Half-Minute Monologues

Read the whole play before you pick your monologue. As you know, that is the only way you can apply the 4 W's to a scene, and a monologue is a section of a scene. You need two monologues exactly two-and-a-half-minutes long. A page and a half of dialogue will eventually play in about two-and-a-half minutes. One monologue should have a serious mood about it. The other monologue can have a lighthearted mood. Don't worry about a monologue coming to a dramatic conclusion. Pick a beginning that will establish your character; use the rest of the monologue to establish a few of the dimensions of that character. If you need to cut the monologue so that it will play in two and a half minutes, cut thoughts and images out of the monologue here and there. Don't cut passages that will destroy the train of thought. Keep passages to which you can score for specific actors' work. Most auditioners will limit your entire audition to five minutes. If you begin to run over the time period, they will cut you off and you may have lost your chance to do some of your best actors' work.

Blocking an Audition Monologue

You will probably audition in an empty studio or on a bare stage or inside a set of a production in progress. Ignore the set if it is there. Find an empty space downstage in good light. The only furniture you can allow yourself is one straight-backed chair. If you are going to use a chair and one isn't immediately available, before you introduce yourself ask where you can find one. Go and get it yourself. A chair can be used as a chair on which your character will sit for a short time or as a platform on which he or she can stand. Never have your character sit down through an entire audition monologue. A chair can also be used to physically locate a character to whom your character is speaking. If you use the chair to sit or stand on, don't use it for the character to whom you are speaking. Never expect more than one chair to be available.

A character to whom your character is speaking should be a specific personalization. Whether or not you use a chair to locate a character to whom your character is speaking, you should imagine that character to be sitting or standing on the downstage edge of the acting area about three feet to one side of a point that is directly in front of your auditioner or auditioners. If there are two characters, and there should be no more than two to whom your character is speaking, put the second personalization of a character on the downstage edge of the acting area three feet in the opposite direction of the first character. Any character to whom your character is speaking must be facing upstage so that you never upstage your-

107

self when you are talking to your personalization of a character. Locate and maintain the height from the floor of the eyes of the character to whom you are speaking.

Find Ways for Your Character to Move

When you rehearse your monologue, you should stage it so that your character has a chance to move fairly frequently in the acting space. That space should be no more than twelve feet wide by six feet deep. You might not audition in a studio or on stage. You may have to audition in someone's cramped office or in a hotel room.

As you score your monologue, put people, places and events to which your character refers up and out front of the acting area. Score in places where your character visualizes or physically refers to those people, places and events. Give yourself a focus for your sense-memories that will make your reactions to those memories available to you and the auditioners.

Let your intentions and your actions move you away or toward your sense-memories and the character or characters to whom your character is speaking. If there are two characters to whom your character is speaking, you have a nice opportunity to move back and forth between them. If one of the people or things to which your character refers is a pleasant experience up and out left and another reference that is unpleasant is up and out right, you have the opportunity to have your character move back and forth between those two references and to play one off against the other. Don't, however, be perpetually on the move. If you use a chair to sit or stand on, let your character settle for a few beats and connect to a strong sense-memory or inner monologue.

Keep Alive but Not Busy

Just because your character is not moving doesn't mean that he is not alive. Very unpleasant or pleasant sense-memories, strong intentions and inner monologues are what bring the playwright's words and your character's facial expressions and body language alive and available to the audience. Don't pick a passive, introspective, thoughtful monologue. Pick an interesting, lively monologue that will put the dimensions of your character into action and capture the attention of your auditioner or auditioners.

Fulfill the 4 W's without Objects and with Limited Activity

Don't use actual objects to create an activity for your monologue. If you are going to fulfill an activity, make it a brief, simple activity. Limit yourself to one object and do a thorough job of physicalizing that object. The student who auditioned for New York University physicalized and picked a daisy and plucked off its petals one by one. The activity made a dramatic statement and it did not detract from the character's through line of intention in the monologue.

Physicalization has trained you to bring alive actual objects and to appreciate the multidimensional life of those objects. An auditioner, however, doesn't want to play guessing games about what the object may be that an actor is physicalizing. The auditioner wants to see how your body, unencumbered with objects and activity, works to bring a character alive. He or she wants to hear you bring the playwright's words alive. If an object is essential to the action, and you physicalize it, don't leave any questions in an auditioner's mind about what that object is.

Manifesting All the 4 W's

Know specifically who your character is. Don't be afraid to manifest his specific physical states of being. Know where your character is and where he came from and where he may be going. Know what time of day it is and the specific weather conditions. Most importantly, know what your character's intentions are. Manifest all the 4 W's to the extent that they will help bring your character alive but use intention as the through line of action to which to attach all your actors' work. Don't ever, in an audition monologue, have your character "sort of want" what he thinks he might want; know what your character *needs* and go for it.

Come from somewhere into the place where the monologue takes place or take a moment before you begin the monologue to connect to where your character is. Then, connect yourself moment to moment to what you have rehearsed. Fulfill each beat and allow your character to make transitions between beats. Stay alive, relaxed and connected, especially to your character's intention.

Go Into Action as Quickly as Possible

When auditioners call you into the acting space to do your monologues, waste no time getting started. Prepare before you come into the acting space. When you arrive, you should be physically and vocally warmed up and physically and mentally relaxed. You should be ready to connect yourself to the first beat of action or doing in the monologue.

Before you introduce yourself, if you are going to use a chair, put it where you want it. Then, step in front of your auditioner or auditioners. Stand in alignment not less than six feet away from the audition people. Relax, breathe to your bellows, and with good resonation and articulation, tell them your name and the titles of the plays from which you have taken your monologues. Let them know that you will go from one monologue to the next with only a brief moment of transition. Then, get in place to begin, quickly but gently free your head with the seven vertebrae, let gravity have your arms, breathe to your bellows and begin.

When you have finished your first monologue, say "Scene." Move your chair if you need to move it. Get in place to begin the next monologue. Do a quick relaxation. Connect to the first beat and begin. When you have finished your second monologue say "Scene." Then, step in front of your auditioners and say "Thank you" and mean it and leave. If the auditioners want to comment on your work let them do it of their own accord. Don't ask them to comment. When you have finished, take the attitude that you have done the best you could do and that the auditioners will recognize this, if not immediately, then in their own good time.

If you have done your work thoroughly and committed yourself moment to moment to your work, you will have given an audition of which you can be proud. You will have impressed your auditioners.

UNIVERSITIES AND COLLEGES

Selecting an Undergraduate Program

There are many universities nationwide that have undergraduate theatre departments where actors' training programs can give you the training and experience necessary to begin a professional career as an actor. Most of the theatre departments in these schools have a close affiliation with a nearby professional regional theatre. A BFA degree in acting from such a school will be respected by professional theater people. One of these universities in the Northeast has a program that farms out its acting students to one of the half dozen top professional studios in New York City. These grand old professional studios are headed by the teachers who founded them and who have trained many of the best American actors of the last fifty years. Unless you are lucky, however, you won't study at first with the head of the studio. You will study with one of his or her assistants. Then, if you are good enough, after a year or two you may study with the teacher who founded the studio.

Acceptance into the undergraduate programs that can train you to begin a professional career can be a problem. They are very competitive. You will not only have to audition as an actor for acceptance into the theatre department, you will also have to meet all the requirements of the undergraduate college of which the theatre department is a part. You will be required to have top high school grades, high SAT scores and an impressive list of extracurricular activities.

If I had my choice of the programs at any of the respected university theatre departments, I would pick a program whose training would help me create believable multidimensional, human characters. I would audit exercise and scene classes.

Some scene classes in theatre departments in very good universities are taught in the sink-or-swim theory of actors' training. The theory is that if you do a lot of scenes, you will learn a lot about acting. I say that theory is pure nonsense. The only way you can learn to create characters and to build roles in a variety of dramatic forms and periods of style is to take your time preparing each scene. Quantity is never a substitute for quality.

Also, if I had a choice of programs, I would ask about classes in the disciplines associated with actors' training, such as vocal production, singing, dancing, etc. I would attend one of the theatre department's productions. I would find out if untrained freshmen were cast in department productions. I would want to know if the actors' work in the productions supported the actors' training given by the department. Sometimes, strangely enough, the training is forgotten as soon as performing in a production begins. If I saw demonstrational, mechanical acting in a department production, I would be very suspicious about the actors' training available at that school.

As I have said, some of the undergraduate schools I have been describing try to prepare their acting students to begin professional acting careers. Most undergraduate theatre departments, however, will only give you an introduction to actors' training. They will advise you to go to a graduate school or to a regional theatre conservatory for further training.

If You Don't Need a Professional Acting Career, Stop Preparing for One

If you don't feel you *need* to be a professional actor, change your plans. Don't waste your time and money. Make acting an avocation rather than a vocation. Use your university hours to study for another profession and go to private studio classes on the side. If you aren't consumed with the ambition and drive to become a professional actor, you won't make it. At the very moment that you are reading this sentence, not more than ten per cent of the membership in the actors' unions — AEA, SAG and AFTRA — have acting jobs.

REGIONAL THEATRE CONSERVATORIES AND PRIVATE STUDIOS

If you can't get into a good graduate program or you don't have the money to attend graduate school, then look for a good regional theatre conservatory program or a good private studio.

Some regional theatre conservatories will give you the same thorough training and performance experience a graduate school could give you. Conservatories want their applicants to have undergraduate degrees but not necessarily degrees in theatre. These conservatories, however, have only been in existence for a few years. They haven't had the time to establish reputations that the graduate schools have had. You will have to look at their programs very carefully. Also, conservatory programs will work you more than eight hours a day, at least six days a week.

If you have a profession outside of the theatre and you can't afford the time to go to a conservatory or if you want good scene classes but you don't want to join an institution to get them, find a good private studio class. Private studio classes, even the grand old studios in New York City, will take you without any degrees or even previous acting experience. To get into the Actors Studio in New York City, however, you will have to pass the toughest auditions ever given an actor, but if you get in, you will be a member for life and for free. There is now an Actors Studio West in Hollywood. The better the private studio and the closer the studio is to New York City or Hollywood, the tougher getting into the studio will be.

Many of the regional theatre conservatories use professional actors, stage managers and directors from the regional theatres with which they are affiliated as their acting teachers. Many of these teachers run private studio scene classes on the side, outside the conservatories. Some of the teachers in these private studios across the country are as good as the best teachers in the grand old studios in New York City. They often offer scene classes for teen-agers and for people who want to study acting as an avocation and not a vocation.

MAKING THE RIGHT CHOICES

Choosing a Class

If the work given in this book is the work you would like to do to train yourself to be a good actor, then use this book as a yardstick for measuring the standards of any scene class or actors' training program. I believe this book presents a technique that will establish a style of acting for you that will serve you very well in all dramatic forms and all period styles of theatre.

Most graduate schools will teach you a number of styles of acting, some of which will contradict what I am teaching you in this book. That can be very confusing. If you like the technique of acting this book presents, then look for scene classes that will give you a chance to reinforce the work this book presents.

Each of the grand old studios in New York City will emphasize one or more of the aspects of the work in this book. I have tried to give you the best of what all of the founders of the grand old studios has to offer.

Choosing a Teacher

If you want to continue the work presented in this book, no matter whether you are going to study in a college or a university, a conservatory or a private studio, it is important to find the right scene teacher.

You are not ready as yet to give a performance; therefore, find a scene teacher who will not immediately demand performance level work from you. In a beginning scene class, you need a teacher who will help you apply actors' work to a text, not a teacher who is a frustrated director or actor who needs immediate results from his or her students. Teachers who point out positive moments in their students work and then work on specific moments that need work are the best kind. Teachers who give only general or negative criticism are to be avoided.

A teacher may not use exactly the same terminology that you use but if you are talking about the same actors' process, you will soon solve the language barrier. The atmosphere of the class should be friendly and constructive. If the students in a class are relaxed and concentrate on their work and they are working carefully and easily, they can become the sort of supportive audience and scene partners you are looking for. You can count on the fact that if you let them know first what was good about their work and then let them know how you think their work could be improved, they will return the favor. Your fellow students can often be your best teachers. If the only one who gives feedback to the students is the teacher and that feedback is doctrinaire and not open to questioning or if there is a lot of backbiting and jealousy-motivated criticism flying around the class, you have the wrong class and the wrong teacher. Keep trying. There are many good teachers to be found.

Choosing a Scene

Once you have found the right class and the right teacher, don't just sit and watch. Get to work immediately. Use the experience you have had preparing your audition monologues. You can be secure in the fact that you have a technique. You know what actors' work is. Now, to find a scene that fits.

First of all, you need a scene that doesn't present unnecessary challenges. You need a scene that will help you to use yourself to create a multidimensional character, a scene that will help you create a basic character-to-character relationship. You don't need a scene that develops into a character-to-character conflict and, therefore, asks for an emotional release from your character. You don't need a scene that asks you to create a character whose age, personality and experience in life are entirely different from yours. You don't need a scene that asks you to create a comedy character you think has to be funny. The sort of scene I have in mind usually comes at the beginning of a play — an expository scene.

To begin, find scenes in twentieth-century plays that take place in the twentieth century. Study the list in the Dramatic Form section of this book. Every play has its own style but plays written before the twentieth century or plays about periods of style before the twentieth century will make demands on you that you should not consider until later.

By all means, use your teacher's and fellow students' advice in choosing a scene. Use one of the many collections of scene books but don't work on a scene without reading the whole play.

Published screenplays are hard to find; not many libraries or bookstores carry them, but, if you have access to screenplays, you can probably find a good expository scene in one of them.

Don't Copy Another Actor's Work

By all means, pick an expository scene from a favorite movie but don't try to do a scene from a movie or a play the way your favorite actor did the scene. Fine acting is not a form of mimicry. Remember that the first step in fine acting is learning to use yourself in creating a character. Your favorite actor does not have the same storehouse of sense-memories that you have. Your storehouse of sense-memories is your very own special scource of creative imagination. You will want to use your own creative imagination, not somebody else's, to create characters.

Don't Repeat Your Previous Work on a Character

Just for the sake of your getting started to work, or for your having an immediate success experience in your scene class, don't immediately work on a scene or a character on which you have previously worked. More than likely, after having worked your way through the Building a Technique section of this book, you now have, in at least some ways, a different approach to your actors' work. Use the technique you have developed. Give it a chance. If you trust the work I have taught you, it will work for you. Later, when you have confidence that this technique works and you have used it to create a number of characters you have never worked on before then, by all means, recreate a character you played in the past. I think you will be surprised at the new multidimensionality of the character. You will also be surprised at the ease with which this character lives moment to moment within the dramatic event of the play.

Choosing a Scene Partner

For your first few scenes work on two-character, not three- or four-character scenes. You are going to have to work with your scene partner outside of class and it is difficult enough to get together as often as you should with one scene partner, let alone two or three. There is never enough time in class to do the extensive work you should be doing. Your first prerequisite in choosing a scene partner is to find someone who wants to work as carefully and as thoroughly as you want to work.

Before you pick a scene partner, get to know the person. Go out for coffee; talk to each other. Don't hesitate to ask a potential partner about his process of working. The fact that he will use the same or a different process than you is not as important as whether you feel he will respect your process of work. Start to discuss a particular scene. Ask your potential partner how he would start to work on the scene. If he immediately begins to talk like a director and begins to talk results, if he begins to tell you how the scene should be done and how your character should behave, find another scene partner.

At the very least you want someone who is willing to do some improvisational work and to work in the beginning without preconceived ideas of what will happen in the scene and especially who your character is going to be. You want your character and the dramatic event to develop layer by layer. You want a chance to develop all the 4 W's of the scene.

Read the Whole Play

Never start to work on a scene without reading the whole play. The through line of action of the play will help you determine the through line of intention for your character. The dialogue and the italics, usually in parentheses, will give you hints about who your character is and who he was before the action of the play began to take place. More than likely, you will find out from a thorough reading of the play what your character does for a living, where he lives, when the action takes place, and what your character was doing just before the scene takes place.

RESEARCH AND PERIOD STYLE

The dialogue and the italics will give you some of the facts about the 4 W's of your character but you need more information than this. You must fill in the outline. You must use your sense-memory imagination, your acquaintance with people who remind you of your character, and your experience with the style of life your character lives. What you can't imagine from your own sense-memory experiences you are going to have to research. You must develop a clear sense-memory picture of all the 4 W's:

WHO: The mental attitude and depth of feeling, social milieu, work and play, family, friends, clothes your character wears, social manners, physical mannerisms, thoughts and memories of people, places and things of times past.

WHERE: The environs, the town or city in which your character lives, the house, the workplace, the play places — what he sees when he looks out a window of the place where the scene takes place — what he knows is in the next room, upstairs, downstairs, what is outside, north, east, west and south of where the scene takes place.

WHEN: The time of day or season in which the scene takes place and the year, the era, the period style of the time of the play.

WHAT: What your character wants or needs out of life, his psychological objective and what he wants or needs within the time frame of the play, his through line of intention, what he does to get what he wants or needs.

Periods of Style

I have said that every play has its own style and that is because no play is about exactly the same people, living in exactly the same place at exactly the same time, with exactly the same style of life as the people in another play. There are, of course, numbers of plays that may take place during the same general period of style.

I define a period of style with the dominant characteristics of the style of life of the majority of a particular group of people living during a fairly specific time in history. During this time period the group thinks, behaves, expresses itself and dresses a good deal differently than it did during a previous period of time.

Every play has its own style and that is because no play is about exactly the same people, living in exactly the same place at exactly the same time with exactly the same style of life. (Author Carlton Colyer, right, as Shep and Stephen Eliot as Manley in The Disenchanted *by Budd Schulberg and Harvey Breit.)*

During the twentieth century the dominant style of life of people living in the West has changed approximately every ten years. Even the dominant style of life of people living in the same town, in the same house, with the same family has changed from what it was ten years ago.

If you find this hard to believe, look at family albums. Talk to family and friends who were your age ten years ago. To find out what the majority of the people did and how they dressed ten years ago, look at ten-year-old pictorial magazines. You can find back copies of *Life, Seventeen, Look, House and Garden* and other magazines in the periodical section of most libraries. Look at films or television shows made ten years ago that are about people living in the style of life predominant then.

Today, styles in clothes change more often than every ten years. The people who set styles in clothes can communicate and manipulate changes in fashion whenever they choose to do so. The ownership of more and more television sets by more and more of the world's families makes this possible.

Before the twentieth century, a major war or the collapse or emergence of a major world empire usually marked the change in a period of style. Predominant styles of life in the West lasted from approximately forty years to as long as five hundred years in the case of the Middle Ages. Two periods of style in the twentieth century were marked by World War I and World War II but today it is the ever increasing speed of communications that dictates the pace of changes of style.

With this in mind, even when doing a twentieth century play, be careful; research the style of life of a character about whom you have little or no firsthand knowledge.

Doing Research to Play a Role

When I did the play *The Disenchanted,* I only had six days of rehearsal to create my character and to build my role of Shep Sterns. Shep is a nineteen-year-old writer who has accompanied a famous writer of the 1920s, Manley Halliday, to New York City and Webster College to help him write a movie script about a winter Mardi Gras at the college. It was obvious to me that the proper names used in the play were thin disguises for actual people and places.

Perhaps the best scene in the play is the 1920s versus the 1930s argument that the two writers have. Halliday is unable to work and Sterns, faced with a deadline for the movie script, is panicked. Halliday begins to speak with nostalgia of his need for the inspiration of the Golden Age of the '20s, and Sterns tells him that there is no inspiration to be found there. He says that the 1920s are responsible for all the problems the country is having in the 1930s. He wants to get back to reality and to write a script.

Because I was doing another job up until the time I reported for rehearsals for *The Disenchanted,* I had not done any work on the play. I knew, however, that, even though I had very little time to do my research, in order to come alive as Shep Sterns, I needed to know more about the '20s and the '30s. I was born in 1930 so I knew the era from the point of view of a child. I needed to know the '20s and '30s from the point of view of a young man born in 1920.

In between rehearsals and learning my lines, I went to a nearby college library and did what research I could, but I have always felt cheated that I didn't have the chance to do the thorough job of research I felt I needed to do.

With all this in mind, I took the opportunity recently to research the two periods and to write sketches of them to show you the sort of research an actor should do on the period of style or periods of style involved in a play in which the actor is building a role.

How to Research Twentieth Century Periods of Style

I had fun. I started with *The 1987 Information Please Almanac* (Houghton Mifflin, Boston, 1987) and Bernard Grun's *The Timetables of History* (based on Werner Stein's *Kulturfahrplan,* A Touchstone Book, Simon and Schuster, New York, 1982). The almanac's "Headline History" section gave highlights of the politics and economy of the times in question. *The Timetables of History* is one of the few reference books that lists events of daily life, the arts, science, philosophy, religion, etc.

When I found a person or an event I wanted to know more about I turned to *The New Columbia Encyclopedia* (Columbia University Press, New York, 1975) as well as books on art, architecture, interior design, music, theatre and movies. I reread two novels — one set in the period style of the '20s and one set in the '30s. I read the biography *Zelda* by Nancy Milford (Avon Books, New York, 1970), which gave me details of the style of life of Zelda and Scott Fitzgerald. I watched a couple of movies that dramatized the style of life of the times.

Most costume books have very little about fashions in dress in the twentieth century. A costume designer friend of mine, however, put me on to *A History of Fashion* by J. Anderson Black, Madge Gorland, and Frances Kennett (Morrow, New York, 1980). The book does a thorough job of describing and illustrating men's and women's fashions from 1900 to 1980. Other good sources of twentieth century fashions in clothes are *The New York Times* magazine sections, "Fashions in Men's (Women's) Clothes" and the advertisements in magazines of the period under research. Any good library has microfilm of back issues of newspapers and magazines.

After I had read about the '20s and '30s, looked at pictures, watched movies, and listened to and danced to the music of the times, I wanted to go back and recreate Shep Sterns and to do the play, *The Disenchanted,* again. I had sensory images and thoughts and feelings with which to work that I hadn't had when I had played the role. After this research I was ready to create a truly multidimensional character.

The sketches of the style of life in the '20s and '30s in the United States that follow are written from the research I have done. If you have decided to do a play set in the '20s or '30s, they are not meant to do your work for you. They are meant as an example of the sort of research you should do.

Sketches of the Style of Life in the U.S. in the 1920s and 1930s from an Actor's Research Point of View

The Jazz Age or the Roaring Twenties in the United States was a time of prosperity and celebration. While Europe suffered from economic instability and labor unrest after World War I, America thrived on the stable dollar and low manufacturing and consumer prices. The Republican administrations of Warren Harding and Calvin Coolidge protected and encouraged big business.

John Scopes was found guilty of teaching evolutionary theory and was fined and jailed.

Prohibition encouraged rather than discouraged drinking and gangsters flourished on rum running. Gang warfare came to a dramatic climax with the St. Valentine's Day Massacre in Chicago in 1929. In 1927, corruption and cronyism in government was uncovered in the Teapot dome scandal, the fraudulent selling of naval oil resources.

Benito Mussolini established a fascist government in Italy and very few people outside of Germany took the strutting, howling Adolf Hitler seriously. In Russia, the Red Army was triumphant over the White Armies. Lenin died; Leon Trotsky was exiled and Joseph Stalin took over the Communist Party.

In the United States, the flourishing economy suddenly collapsed. Profit taking and speculation on credit brought on the stock market crash on Black Friday in October 1929. Banks failed. People lost their savings and their homes. Businesses failed. The Depression set in.

Fashions in Clothes:

Men wore wide-collared, double-breasted and single-breasted jackets shaped to the waist with side seams. Trousers, sometimes called Oxford bags, were wide, unpleated and cuffed. Overcoats were long and double-breasted. Raccoon coats were worn on football weekends. Narrow-brimmed felt trilbies, bowlers and homburgs were the hats for formal wear. Blue blazers, grey flannels and straw boaters or checked wool jackets, plus fours and wool caps were worn on informal occasions. Two-toned brogues with pointed toes were the formal and informal footwear. Most men's hair was cut semi-short and parted at the side. A few men flashed the gigolo or polished look, hair slicked straight back with no part in it.

Women wore straight tubular dresses belted at the hips. In the early 1920s the hemline was just below the knee. Later it was above the knee and rolled stockings were revealed when women sat down. The corset, the waistline and the bustline disappeared. Pleated skirts made of fluttering crêpe de chine or chiffon flowed as women danced. That's how women of the 20s came to be known as flappers. In 1924 "Coco" Gabriel Chanel ushered in the garconne or undeveloped adolescent look, hair worn in an Eton crop and parted at the side, a cloche hat enveloping the head and concealing the forehead.

Very wide-brimmed, low-crowned hats were worn in the summertime. Sharply pointed leather shoes and fine silk stockings were worn for all occasions. Long strings of pearls or beads, dangling plastic earrings and dozens of slave or service stripe bracelets touched off the flapper look. Some women affected the vamp look inspired by Theda Bara and Pola Negri in their movies. The vamp look was achieved by using very light facial make-up highlighted by eyes outlined with kohl and eyelashes loaded with mascara.

Business, Social Relationships and Manners:

The cocktail party and club life symbolized the social life of the period. The cocktail shaker replaced the tea set. Membership in a country club and men's or women's club was a social prerequisite. Smoking cigarettes in public but not outdoors was a socially acceptable practice for women. In 1920 the Nineteenth Amendment gave women the vote.

Being part of a club was important even in the literary world. The Vicious Circle, a lunch group that met at the Algonquin Hotel in New York City, included Alexander Woolcott, Robert Benchley, Dorothy Parker, Robert Sherwood, Heywood Broun, George S. Kaufman, and sometimes Tallulah Bankhead. This group was considered the crème de la crème of cynical intelligentsia.

Art and Architecture:

New York's Empire State Building, George Washington Bridge and Holland Tunnel were built in the 1920s. Frank Lloyd Wright, a student of the great Louis Sullivan, designed poured concrete houses in basic geometric shapes that echoed the surroundings of those houses. His use of glass opened up fluid inner spaces and related them to the exterior.

Expressionism and surrealism ruled the art world. Max Ernst is considered the father of surrealism. The early expressionism of Paul Klee's "Twittering Machine" and Marc Chagal's "Lover's Bouquet" has a whimsical innocence about it. Eduard Munch's "The Shriek" and "The Kiss" are violent and emotionally charged. Wassily Kandinsky is considered the originator of abstract expressionism.

For a sense of city life of the 1920s, see the paintings of John Sloan of the Ashcan School such as "Sixth Avenue and Third Street."

The climax of the art nouveau spirit was expressed in Louis Tiffany's glassware and lamps, but art nouveau designs quickly gave way to the new art deco inspired by studies in aerodynamics and new materials such as chrome and plastic.

Interior Decoration:

Opulence was the byword of the furnishings displayed at the Paris National Exposition in 1925. Inlaid wood richly trimmed with fur, leather, aluminum, or chrome was the new medium in art deco furniture design. Fluorescent lamps produced general lighting with less shadow. Venetian blinds became popular.

Communications and Transportation:

In 1920 the first airmail was flown from New York City to San Francisco. In 1927 Charles A. Lindberg flew solo from New York City to Paris. Westinghouse in the United States and the BBC in England were the first radio broadcasting stations. In 1924 the Model T Ford with its horse and buggy body and its wooden spoke wheels sold for less than $300.00.

Entertainment:

Automation in both agriculture and manufacturing brought more leisure time into the lives of the working class and the lower middle class. In the 1920s very few forms of public entertainment were prohibited to anybody because of price. Everyone could go to see silent movies at the nickelodeon or play jazz records on their Victrola, which was manually wound up. Jack Dempsey and Gene Tunney, heavyweight boxing champions, and Babe Ruth, who hit sixty home runs for the New York Yankees in 1927, were the professional sports heroes. Bobby Jones ruled the golf links and Helen Wills and Jack Tilden the tennis courts. Huge concrete stadiums, such as the Yale Bowl and England's Wembley Stadium, were built.

There were many crazes such as the board game Mah Jong, marathon dancing, miniature golf, and flagpole sitting. Crossword puzzles became popular. In 1925 Harold Vanderbilt devised the card game contract bridge.

After Storyland's houses of prostitution in New Orleans were closed down by the U.S. Navy, the Dixieland jazz musicians who had played in the houses moved north and made Chicago the capital city of jazz. The best of the jazz band music of the '20s was Louis Armstrong's "Basin Street Blues," Kid Ory's "Society Blues," and Bix Beiderbeck's "Tiger Rag." Meade Lux Lewis' "Honky Tonk Train Blues" is a good example of boogie woogie.

In the early 1920s the Charleston was the most popular dance but by 1927 the fox trot was more in fashion. All through the '20s the tango brought passionate romance to the dance floor.

Irving Berlin's *Music Box Reviews,* Jerome Kern's and Oscar Hammerstein's *Show Boat,* George Gershwin's *Lady Be Good* and *Funny Face,* Richard Rodgers' and Lorenz Hart's *Connecticut Yankee,* and Jerome Kern's *Sally* were the top Broadway musicals of the time.

Oskar Straus' *Intermezzo,* Richard Strauss' *The Last Waltz,* and Sigmund Romberg's *Blossom Time* were the top operettas.

Some of the Popular Songs of the '20s:
"Tea for Two," "Show Me the Way to Go Home," "Desert Song," "Blue Room," "Ol' Man River," "My Blue Heaven," "Blue Skies, "Crazy Rhythm," "Making Whoopee," "Stardust," and "Singing in the Rain."

The 1920s proved a golden age for literature. The expressionsim of the times can be found in the following strongly symbolic novels: Franz Kafka's *The Trial,* Herman Hesse's *Steppenwolf,* James Joyce's *Ulysses,* William Faulkner's *The Sound and the Fury,* Thomas Mann's *The Magic Mountain,* D. H. Lawrence's *Women in Love,* and E. M. Forster's *Passage to India.*

Novels of the '20s that Best Describe the Style of Life of the Time:
Evelyn Waugh's *Decline and Fall,* F. Scott Fitzgerald's *The Great Gatsby,* Theodore Drieser's *An American Tragedy,* Sinclair Lewis' *Main Street,* Thomas Wolfe's *Look Homeward Angel,* and Ernest Hemingway's *The Sun Also Rises.*

The poetry of T. S. Eliot, especially "The Wasteland," is full of images of the time.

Many American writers, known as The Lost Generation, lived for a time during the '20s as expatriots in Paris.

The Psychology and Philosophy of the Times Is Expressed in:
C. G. Jung's *Psychological Types,* Sigmund Freud's *The Ego and the Id* and Bertrand Russell's *The Analysis of Mind.*

Theatrical Modes:
Constantin Stanislavsky and the Moscow Art Theatre toured Europe and the Americas from 1922 to 1924. Two members of the company, Richard Boleslavsky and Maria Ouspenskaya, stayed behind in the United States and taught acting at the American Laboratory Theatre.

Dramatic Form:
A few of the expressionistic plays of the '20s: Eugene O'Neill's *The Emperor Jones* and *The Great God Brown,* Elmer Rice's *The Adding Machine,* and Jean Giradoux's *Amphitryon '38.*

Plays that Dramatize the Style of Life of the '20s:
Philip Barry's *Holiday,* Noel Coward's *Private Lives,* Elmer Rice's *Street Scene,* and Sidney Howard's *They Knew What They Wanted.* Realism became the predominant dramatic style.

Movies:
The first talkie, *The Jazz Singer* with Al Jolson, came out in 1927. The first Mickey Mouse cartoon was produced in 1928. Some of the classic silent movie farces of the 1920s are: Charlie Chaplin's *The Kid* and *The Gold Rush,* Harold Lloyd's *Why Worry* and *The Freshman,* and Buster Keaton's *The Navigator.*

Epic silent films are Fred Niblo's *Ben-Hur* and Cecil B. De-Mille's *The King of Kings.* Fine performances are given by John Barrymore in *Don Juan* and Greta Garbo in *Flesh and the Devil.* Rudolf Valentino's *The Sheik* and *The Son of the Sheik* were the most popular movies of the '20s.

1930-1939

The 1930s were the depression years. In the United States the time was marked by as much as one-third of the work force being unemployed. In the early 1930s, city men sold apples on street corners. Families stood in soup kitchen lines. A drought in the Southwest and bank takeovers of farm property forced farm families to migrate. Oakies, as they were called, strapped their possessions to their farm trucks and headed to the promised land of California. When they got there they found that there wasn't enough work for all of them. When they set up campsites, the police moved them on.

Many academics and artists were professed socialists. Cells of communist sympathizers were formed throughout the country.

Republican President Herbert Hoover's Reconstruction Finance Corporation that provided low interest government loans to banks and railroads failed to stimulate the economy.

The election of Democratic President Franklin D. Roosevelt ultimately proved that a strong benevolent federal government can effect the greatest good for the greatest number of people. The plan Roosevelt put into action came to be known as the New Deal. Step by step the New Deal brought the United States out of the Depression.

Meanwhile, manevolent fascist governments in Europe and Asia were preparing to bring the greatest harm possible to the greatest number of people. The Nazi propaganda machine pushed the world over the abyss into World War II. They promised the Germans work and good wages and the return of their national pride that had been taken from them in the Treaty of Versailles after World War I. The Fascists promised to save the world from the red scourge. Big business and the landed aristocracy were afraid communism would take away their wealth. Organized religion feared communist atheism. The Fascists promised to destroy the Communists.

From 1936 to 1939 a preliminary round of World War II was fought in the Spanish Civil War. General Francisco Franco overthrew an elected Republican government and established a dictatorship. In 1936 the Rome-Berlin axis was formed to be joined later by Japan. Nazi propaganda screamed for lebensraum or free space for German expansion. A nonagression pact was signed with Russia. Russia invaded Finland. The Japanese occupied Manchuria and invaded China. Mussolini took Ethiopia and Hitler, having been given the right to partition Czechoslovakia in the Munich Pact, also invaded Poland. World War II had begun.

Fashions in Clothes:

The disorder the world was in was reflected in the confusion of thought in fashion. The 1930s fashions for women began with an increase in femininity. Hair was grown longer in a shingle cut that came half way down the ears. Tiny hats were worn tilted back to reveal the forehead. Skirts were lengthened to mid-calf. Dresses were belted at the waist and curved to fit the waist. There was a slight rounding of the bustline and dresses had a draped decollatage usually adorned with a simulated diamond clip.

Elsa Schiaparelli, however, soon contradicted the feminine look with a mascline trend in design. The Italian designer added broad padded shoulders to short fitted jackets. Epaulettes gave emphasis to tiny waistlines. Jackets of hyacinth or pink tweed were matched to brown or black wool dresses and skirts.

Sunbathing became very popular and Schiaparelli designed beach trousers with bell-bottoms and flap fronts to be worn with loose, short coats of crêpe du chine or shantung. Hand knitted one piece bathing suits and big floppy hats were also fashionable beach wear.

Late in the 1930s women's hair was grown longer at the back and caught up in a net or brushed up on top of the head. For the first time retailers sold coordinated collections of bags, gloves and shoes. Gloves were always a part of the ensemble and nylon stockings came on the market. Girls wore ankle socks and saddle shoes to school.

Men's jackets became looser but still fitted. Lapels were broader and trousers were straight cut and slimmer than the baggy pants of the '20s. Overcoats were usually single-breasted rather than double-breasted. Men's hair was still worn short but it had a softer look, and it was held in place with a little dab of Brill Cream.

Business, Social Relationships and Manners:

Japan tried to conquer the world's consumer market by making cheap copies of Western manufactured goods. The 21st Amendment repealed Prohibition. The biggest social event of the age was the abdication of Edward VIII of England to marry the American divorcee, Mrs. Wallis Simpson. Edward's brother was crowned George VI and Edward and Mrs. Simpson became the Duke and Duchess of Windsor.

Bohemian artists settled in places like Greenwich Village in New York City. They wore smocks and aprons or their work clothes everywhere. Their wearing of French berets connected them to the Lost Generation artists and writers of the '20s.

Art and Architecture:

The major architectural and engineering achievements of the 1930s were the construction of Rockefeller Center and the Lincoln Tunnel in New York City, the Harbor Bridge in Sydney, Australia, the Golden Gate Bridge in San Francisco, and Boulder and Bonneville Dams in Colorado and Utah.

Frank Lloyd Wright had become the leader of the Functional School of architecture. He designed Taliesin West in Phoenix, Arizona, and the Kaufman House at Bear Run, Pennsylvania. In 1938 the International School, the Functional School and art deco design came together in the buildings and sculptures of the New York World's Fair.

The art most closely associated with the 1930s is the massive sculptural works of Henry Moore and Jacob Epstein, the W.P.A's murals in American post offices, the American primitive work of Grant Wood and Grandma Moses, and Picasso's powerful expressionist painting, "Guernica," that depicts the horrors of the Spanish Civil War.

Interior Decoration:

The aerodynamic lines of art deco aluminum and stainless steel furniture and the glow of fluorescent lighting were still the height of fashionable interior design but most people in the 1930s were more practical than they were fashionable. The furniture in the majority of American homes was sturdily made Grand Rapids plain oak and maple. Walls that were often stuccoed in the California style were painted light colors. Wooden doors and paneling were left bare and varnished. Plain wood bookcases were built into the walls and varnished. Brass sconces, placed on the walls by the builder, were the main sources of light. Full-length curtains were hung at archways and windows. Living room furniture tended to be upholostered but lightly stuffed. Sofas and chairs had low, square backs.

Communication and Transportation:

Trans-Atlantic steamship crossings became available to more travelers with the launchings of the giants: S. S. Normandy, S. S. Queen Mary, and S. S. Queen Elizabeth. Pan American and British Overseas Airways flew regular passenger flights across the Atlantic. Amelia Earhardt was the first woman to fly solo across the Atlantic but she and her plane were lost somewhere in the Pacific Ocean on an attempted around-the-world flight. The German dirigible Hindenberg exploded over Lakehurst, New Jersey, and the disaster was heard live over radio. George VI's coronation was broadcast on radio to a world-wide audience, and Orson Welles' "War of the Worlds" radio broadcast of an imaginary invasion from Mars panicked thousands of listeners and was a dramatic example of the power of public broadcasting.

If you traveled on a passenger train in the U.S. in the '30s, you got where you were going on time. The trip was comfortable and you could eat in a dining car with white linen tablecloths and napkins, a vase with a flower and shining dining car pewterware on your table. A black waiter wearing a white shirt and black bow tie, danced down the aisle with the swaying of the car. He held your meal shoulder high on a tray balanced on the palm of his hand.

In 1938 automobiles still had a high silhouette but they had more sculptured, aerodynamic lines. High hoods, housing big powerful engines, limited the size of windshields which were matched by tiny rear windows. First class letters were sent within the forty eight states with a three cent stamp. Post cards went with a penny stamp.

Entertainment:

The population of the United States was 122 million in 1930. Each week 115 million people went to the movies. Comic strips were at the height of their popularity. Beginning in 1932, the New York Yankees starring Babe Ruth, Lou Gehrig and Joe Dimaggio won six out of eight World Series. In 1931 Bobby Jones won the grand slam of golf, and in 1938, Don Budge won the grand slam of tennis. To Hitler's chagrin, Jesse Owens won four gold medals at the Berlin Olympic Games.

Jazz was still popular in the 1930s. Examples of the best of what was listened to are: Joe Sullivan's "Gin Mill Blues," Jack Teagarden's "Dirty Dog" and Earl Hines' "Down Among the Sheltering Pines." Coleman Hawkins' "Plain Dirt" is known as jive.

Big band swing, however, was the music of the '30s and the '40s. For the best in the sounds of swing of the '30s listen to: Fletcher Henderson's "Queer Notions," Duke Ellington's "Dim-uendo in Blue," Tommy Dorsey's "Marie" with a solo by trumpeter Bunny Berigan, Artie Shaw's "Streamline," Benny Goodman's "King Porter Stomp," Count Basie's "One O'Clock Jump," and Billie Holliday singing on Glenn Miller's recording of "String of Pearls."

The dance step to swing was the lindy. The rhumba bacame popular in 1935 and in England in 1938 they began to do the Lambeth walk.

"The Star Spangled Banner" became the American national anthem in 1931 and one of the popular songs of the times was "God Bless America." Two '30s songs that express the predominant mood of the Depression are: "Brother, Can You Spare a Dime?," and "I Got Plenty of Nuttin',"

Two hit musicals on Broadway were: Cole Porter's *Anyting Goes* and Jerome Kern's *Roberta*.

The most popular radio shows of the 1930s and '40s were: *The Jack Benny Comedy Hour, The Fred Allen Show, The Shadow, The Henry Aldrich Show, The Lone Ranger* and *The Green Hornet.* Children listened to *Jack Armstrong, Captain Midnight* and *Tom Mix* after school. They sent in cereal box tops to *Captain Midnight* and received decoding rings with which they interpreted secret messages at the end of each show. Housewives listened at midday to *Lorenzo Jones and His Wife Belle*.

The novels that best express the spirit of the times were: F. Scott Fitzgerald's *Tender Is the Night,* Erskine Caldwell's *Tobacco Road* and *God's Little Acre,* James T. Farrel's *The Young Lonigan,* and John Steinbeck's *Tortilla Flat* and *The Grapes of Wrath.*

Three non-fictional works that express the thinking of the times were: C. J. Jung's *Psychology and Religion,* John Strachey's *The Theory and Practice of Socialism,* and Andre Malraux's *The Human Condition.*

Theatrical Modes:

A group of young American theatre people all of whom were influenced by their study of Stanislavsky's techniques formed The Group Theatre. Their work on acting technique and ensemble production was to become the main force behind the golden age of American theatre in the 1940s and '50s. Among the group were:

Luther and Stella Adler, Morris Carnovsky, Cheryl Crawford, John Garfield, Elia Kazan, Robert Lewis, Art Smith, Franchot Tone, Lee J. Cobb, Sanford Meisner, Clifford Odets and Lee Strasberg.

Mordecai Gorelic and Lee Simonson, who wrote *The Stage Is Set,* were the scenic designers of the 1930s.

Dramatic Form:

The plays written in the '30s that best portray the life of the times are: Philip Barry's *Philadelphia Story,* Fredrica Lorca's *Blood Wedding,* Elmer Rice's *We the People,* Clifford Odets' *Waiting for Lefty* and *Golden Boy,* Emyln Williams' *The Corn Is Green,* George S. Kaufman's and Lorenz Hart's *You Can't Take It with You,* John Steinbeck's *Of Mice and Men,* Thornton Wilder's *Our Town,* William Saroyan's *The Time of Your Life.* T. S. Eliot's *Murder in the Cathedral* and *The Family Reunion* led the way for the poetic dramas of the 1940s.

Movies:

The 1930s were a golden age of movie making. Films that catch the spirit of the times are: *Grand Hotel* with Greta Garbo and John Barrymore, *Blue Angel* and *Shangrila Express* with Marlene Dietrich, *Anna Christie* with Greta Garbo, *The Big House* with Wallace Beery, *City Lights* and *Modern Times* with Charles Chaplin, *Scarface* and *A Fugitive from a Chain Gang* with Paul Muni, *It Happened One Night* with Clark Gable and Claudette Colbert, *You Can't Take It with You* and *Mr. Smith Goes to Washington* with James Stewart, *The Petrified Forest* with Humphrey Bogart, and *Mr. Deeds Goes to Town* with Gary Cooper and Jean Arthur.

A New Section in Your Storehouse of Sense-Memories

When you compare the style of life in the United States from one decade to the next, you will see that a contemporary society can change radically. Because this is true, you need to know when the play on which you are working takes place. You don't always have to do as much work as I have done to research the lifestyle of a character. Your research will be conditioned by what you know about your character after you have read the entire play. You should realize now the kinds of sources that are available for your research and the sort of information they can provide. You should use this information to build your storehouse of sense-memories to connect to the life of the character you are creating.

Discovering the 4 W's of people you hadn't met before can be a thrilling experience. It is like making new friends. Now you can have the privilege of putting yourself as your character into a style of life you couldn't have lived unless you had done this thorough job of research. It will be like entering a time warp machine and taking a trip into the past.

There is approximately two thousands years of history before the twentieth century about which plays have been written. Eventually, as you create characters in these plays, you will come alive as a citizen of many different specific eras of civilization. When you have done a thorough job of researching the style of life of any period of history, you will not only have a good idea of who your character is and where and when he lives and what he does, you should also know why he does what he does. You will not only have a specific sense of the 4 W's of your character's life; you will also have a sense of the fifth W, why! You will understand the social, psychological and philosophical influences on your character. You can make an educated choice of your character's psychological objective in life that will in turn influence your sense of his through line of intention in the play.

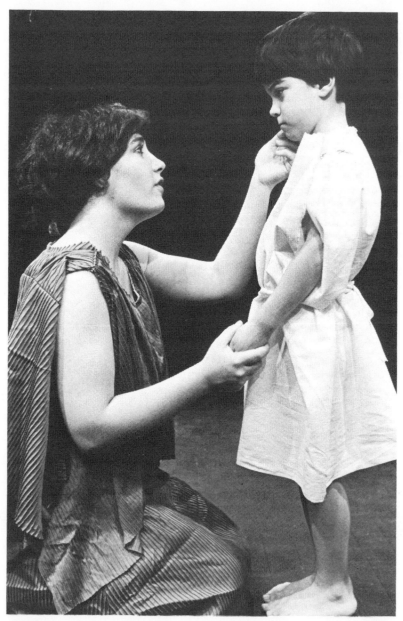

The flaw that brings on the tragic end to the main character in classic tragedy may be in society rather than in the main character. (A scene from Euripides' The Trojan Women, Brown University, Sock and Buskin Theatre.)

2. Building Roles in Different Dramatic Forms

Before you make a definite decision about your character's psychological objective in life and you begin to build his role in the play, you must consider the dramatic form in which the play is written. Plays of the twentieth century are written in seven basic dramatic forms: tragedy, farce, tragicomedy, sentimental comedy, comedy, nonrealism or surrealism, and the absurd. There is an historical precedent for all seven of these dramatic forms. Each form will have a different influence on your choice of the psychological objective for your character and the way in which your character will pursue that objective.

The terms dramatic form, theatrical mode, period style and acting style are often confusing because they are often lumped under one heading: period style. It will be helpful to think of them individually according to their own definitions.

Dramatic Form is the structure and intent of a play. The dramatic form of a play reflects the playwright's attitude about his subject matter.

Theatrical Mode is the way in which a play is staged. It has to do with the relationship of actors to the audience.

Style of acting is the technique of acting that predominates during a particular period of theatrical history.

Period Style has to do with the style of life of the majority of people who lived during the period of human history about which a play is written.

THE FIRST RULES OF CLASSIC TRAGEDY

According to Aristotle, the fourth century B.C. philosopher and drama critic, classic or pure tragedies are serious plays about serious people. Aristotle took as his examples the plays written in the fifth century B.C. by the great Greek tragedians. Aristotle said that in order for them to be pure tragedies these plays must have unhappy endings. The through line of action of these plays must never be interrupted by funny or overly happy moments. The main character must be a hero of major social stature. He has a tragic flaw in his personality. This flaw is the only weakness in his otherwise flawless character. It is inevitable that this flaw will lead the hero to make a mistake that will bring on his tragic downfall. The action of the play must constantly be centered on the hero. There can be no subplots or extra action.

There are a number of twentieth century plays that can be considered classic tragedies. They may not meet all of Aristotle's requirements but they come very close to it. They are serious plays about serious people, but a group of characters may take the place of the one main character. As long as they don't disrupt the through line of action, these plays may contain an occasional happy or even funny moment. The flaw that brings on the tragic end to the main character or group of characters may be in society rather than in the main character or group of characters. The plots of twentieth century tragedies are centered on the main character or group of characters and the lives of these characters always come to unhappy ends. The characters in well-conceived modern tragedies, however, are always multidimensional human beings; whereas the characters in the classic Greek tragedies often were one-dimensional personifications of the idea of a hero.

Best Tragedies Written in the Twentieth Century and Taking Place in the Twentieth Century

Athol Fugard's *A Lesson from Aloes* and *Statements*

Maxim Gorky's *The Lower Depths*

Lillian Hellman's *The Little Foxes, The Children's Hour, Watch on the Rhine, Monserrat* and *Toys in the Attic*

Garcia Lorca's *Blood Wedding, Yerma* and *The House of Bernada Alba*

Arthur Miller's *Death of a Salesman*

Eugene O'Neill's *A Long Day's Journey into Night, Desire Under the Elms* and *Mourning Becomes Electra*

John Pielmeier's *Agnes of God*

Peter Shaffer's *Equus*

John Steinbeck's *Of Mice and Men*

OLD COMEDY, FARCE AND DARK COMEDY

Old comedy is the name given to classic comedies written at the same time as the classic Greek tragedies. Aristophanes' *Lysistrata* is the most famous of the old comedies. All old comedies are farce. They are usually about important, serious subjects, but they take a bawdy, slapstick, lighthearted attitude about life. The actors in old comedy wore character masks that identified the type of character the actor was playing. The behavior of all the characters of old comedy expands human behavior to the point of ridiculousness, but each character's behavior is recognizable as a type of human behavior. There is a traditional type of behavior for each character type. Clever comic servants always make fun of their serious-minded masters, The Doctor, The Soldier or The Merchant. Old comedy farces always have happy endings. *Lysistrata* is a play about women going on a sex strike to stop their warrior husbands from continuing the Pelopponesian War. The warriors finally see the method in their wives' madness and they stop the war.

The Roman playwright Plautus' plays are farce. Commedia dell'arte scenarios, except for their semiromantic interludes, are farce. I call the plays of Moliere and Carlo Goldoni semisocial satire, semifarcical comedies. Carlo Gozzi wrote eighteenth century old comedy farces. The sixteenth century miracle plays are farce. Many of the episodes in Shakespeare's comedies are farcical, but *The Taming of the Shrew, A Comedy of Errors* and *The Merry Wives of Windsor* are the plays of his I would call pure farce.

There aren't many twentieth century plays that are farce but there are some that are superb. In modern farce the actors don't usually wear masks, but the characters are still exaggerated parodies of types of human beings. Sometimes, twentieth century farce plays have strangely serious endings. They often make fun of serious subjects, but they also make fun of forbidden or grotesque subjects. They are usually called dark comedies. They are sometimes included among the plays of the absurd.

Best Farce Written in the Twentieth Century and Taking Place in the Twentieth Century

Christopher Durang's *Sister Mary Ignatius Explains It All for You, The Marrige of Bette and Boo, Beyond Therapy* and *Identity Crisis*

Dario Fo's *The Accidental Death of an Anarchist*

Eugene Ionesco's *Jack or the Submission*

Joe Orton's *Loot, The Ruffian on the Stair, Funeral Games* and *What the Butler Saw*

Plays such as Beth Henley's *Crimes of the Heart,* Sam Shepherd's plays and many of the Theatre-of-the-Absurd plays have farcical moments in them, but it would be a mistake to play any of these plays as pure farce or to think of any of the characters in them as pure farcical characters in the old comedy sense.

TRAGICOMEDY

Because actual life is a wonderful combination of comedy and tragedy, playwrights broke with the classic tragic tradition and wrote tragicomedies. Euripides invented tragicomedy. Aristotle didn't like his plays but Socrates, the great philosopher, said that they were the only plays he would go out of his way to see.

Tragicomedy is about a serious subject and its main characters usually have a serious attitude about life but joyful moments, comic moments, up-beat characters and, most importantly, happy endings can be an important part of tragicomedy.

Most early tragicomedies are melodramatic. Evil characters get what is coming to them, a tragic or unhappy end to their lives. Characters, however, who are basically good but who make an ethical mistake and learn a lesson from this mistake can live happily ever after.

Euripides' *Iphigenia in Tauris* is a story centered on Iphigenia, high priestess of Artemis, who is forced to make human sacrifices to her goddess. She almost sacrifices her long lost brother, Orestes, but there is a happy moment of recognition and reminiscence followed by the fun of their escape from the horrible but dumb King Taos. The play ends with the delightful appearance of the goddess Athena, who brings the melodrama to a satisfying happy ending.

Renaissance playwrights such as Shakespeare and Lope de Vega and the Italians Cinthio, Giambattista Guarini, Torquato Tasso, and Lodovicio Ariosto carried on the tradition Euripides had begun. They wrote melodramatic tragicomedies but they often added the onstage blood and guts moments of dramatic horror of the Roman writer of tragedy, Seneca.

Sometimes these playwrights, especially the seventeenth century tragicomedy playwright Corneille, had to suffer criticism from the neoclassic traditionalists. These traditionalists said that tragedy could only be written the way Aristotle said it should be written. Some of these traditionalists had political power and for awhile they forced playwrights to stop writing tragicomedy. Finally, however, common sense and the audience's fascination with plays that portrayed both the bright side and the dark side of life won out.

The most popular theatre of the nineteenth century was melodramatic tragicomedy and at least half of the best plays of the twentieth century are tragicomedies. Because decorum is seldom a fact of actual life, however, most twentieth century tragicomedies do not concern themselves with a black and white moral code.

Melodrama, nevertheless, is not dead. Joseph Walker's *The River Niger* written and produced in 1973 is a fine example of a grand old melodramatic tragicomedy. Also, many Hollywood movies and serious-minded television shows assume an obligation to punish the bad guys and to have the good guys live happily ever after.

Most of the tragicomedies of today take a nonmelodramatic, realistic outlook on life. They take a generally serious attitude about serious subjects, but they can end on a hopeful, even cheerful, note. The characters of modern tragicomedies are multidimensional human beings who have both their good and bad sides. They may have a lighthearted or a serious attitude about life and they get involved in both happy and unhappy situations.

Best Tragicomedies Written in the Twentieth Century and Taking Place in the Twentieth Century

Maxwell Anderson's and Laurence Stallings' *What Price Glory*
Robert Anderson's *Tea and Sympathy*
Granville Barker's *The Voysey Inheritance*
Phillip Barry's *Hotel Universe*
S. M. Barrie's *Dear Brutus, The Admirable Crichton* and *What Every Woman Knows*
Brendan Behan's *The Hostage*
S. N. Behrman's *Rain from Heaven*
Bertol Brecht's *Mother Courage, Galileo* and *The Good Woman of Setsuan*
Paddy Chayevsky's *Middle of the Night*
Anton Chekhov's *Ivanov*
Michael Christopher's *The Shadow Box*
Caryl Churchill's *Top Girls*
Rose Franken's *Another Language* and *The Coat*
Athol Fugard's *The Blood Knot, Sizwe Bansi Is Dead, "Master Harold"... and the Boys, Hello and Good-Bye* and *The Island*
Christopher Fry's *A Sleep of Prisoners*
John Galsworthy's *Strife, Justice* and *Loyalties*
Michael Gazzo's *A Hatful of Rain*
William Gibson's *The Miracle Worker*
Frank Gilroy's *The Subject Was Roses*
Goodrich and Hackett's *Diary of Anne Frank*
Charles Gordone's *No Place to be Somebody*
Lorraine Hansberry's *A Raisin in the Sun*

David Hare's *Plenty* and *Teeth 'N' Smiles*

Lillian Hellman's *Autumn Garden*

William Hoffman's *As Is*

William Inge's *Come Back Little Sheba, Bus Stop, Picnic, The Dark at the Top of the Stairs* and *A Loss of Roses*

Arthur Laurent's *Home of the Brave*

David Mamet's *American Buffalo, Glen Gary, Glenn Ross* and *Speed the Plow*

Frank Marcus' *The Killing of Sister George*

Arthur Miller's *A View from the Bridge, The Price* and *After the Fall*

Jason Miller's *That Championship Season*

Ferenc Molnar's *Liliom*

Richard Nash's *The Young and the Fair*

Peter Nichols' *National Health* and *Joe Egg*

Marsha Norman's *Getting Out* and *'Night Mother*

Sean O'Casey's *Juno and the Paycock* and *The Plough and the Stars*

Clifford Odets' *Waiting for Lefty, Awake and Sing* and *The Country Girl*

Eugene O'Neill's *Anna Christie, The Iceman Cometh, The Moon for the Misbegotten* and *Strange Interlude*

John Osborne's *A Sense of Detachment, Look Back in Anger, Epitaph for George Dillan* and *The Entertainer*

Miguel Pinero's *Short Eyes*

David Rabe's *Sticks and Bones, Streamers, The Basic Training of Pavlo Hummel, Huryburly* and *In the Boom Boom Room*

Elmer Rice's *We the People* and *Street Scene*

Budd Schulberg's and Harvey Breit's *The Disenchanted*

Peter Shaffer's *Equus* and *Amadeus*

Sam Shepherd's *Curse of the Starving Class, True West, Fool for Love* and *A Lie of the Mind*

Martin Sherman's *Bent*

Robert Sherwood's *Reunion in Vienna, The Petrified Forest* and *Idiot's Delight*

Tom Stoppard's *The Real Thing*

David Storey's *Home* and *The Changing Room*

August Strindberg's *The Dance of Death*

John Millington Synge's *In the Shadow of the Glen*

Ernest Thompson's *On Golden Pond*

Arnold Wesker's *Roots* and *Chips with Everything*

Emlyn Williams' *The Corn Is Green*

Tennessee Williams' *A Streetcar Named Desire, The Glass Menagerie, Summer and Smoke, The Rose Tattoo, Cat on a Hot Tin Roof* and *The Night of the Iguana*

August Wilson's *Ma Rainey's Black Bottom*

NEW COMEDY

In Hellenic times, after Alexander the Great's conquests and before the rise of The Roman Empire, Menander invented what is now called new comedy. His plays took a lighthearted attitude about the semiserious problems of the lives of middle-class people. Menander's plays always ended happily, but they had their serious moments. The behavior of the characters was seldom bawdy or slapstick. The Roman Terence used many of Menander's plot lines to take a lighthearted look at the lives of the Roman middle class, especially the love life of its young gentlemen and the problems they had with their strict fathers. Terence invented the double or parallel plot.

The most popular plays of the seventeenth and eighteenth centuries in England were new comedies, satires of the behavior and morality of the ladies and gentlemen of the upper-middle class. In Restoration and Georgian times, William Congreve, William Wycherly, John Vanbrugh, Richard Brindsley Sheridan and Oliver Goldsmith were the finest of the playwrights of new comedy satire.

Social Satire Should Not Be Done as Farce

Because the characters in these new comedy plays often take what would be today a very lighthearted, frivolous attitude about life and because Moliere's comedies about the seventeenth century French upper-middle class are semifarce conceived in the commedia dell'arte tradition, seventeenth and eighteenth century comedies are often done today as if they were pure old comedy farce. This shows a lack of common sense and a sloppy job of research. Moliere's plays are semifarce but they are also semisocial satires. His characters are not overexaggerated parodies of types of people. Their behavior sometimes may be ridiculous or farcical, even slapstick, but they should also be believably multidimensional human beings.

The characters in Restoration and Georgian comedies may lead frivolous lives but they are human beings of a specific period of style of the past who take their silly social pursuits very seriously. These people flirted, gossiped, gamed and fought duels with a vengeance. Sheridan's plays incorporate some of the serious, sentimental attitudes of the emerging merchant or business class of his time. The social code permitted ladies and gentlemen of seventeeth and eighteenth century England to say bawdy things if they said them cleverly. Bawdy gestures and behavior in public, however, were considered bad manners. City people, both servants and masters, prided themselves on the gracefulness of their behavior. People from the country, on the other hand, might very well behave in a clumsy, oafish manner. Obviously, a thorough job of research should be done before attempting to create a character from seventeenth or eighteenth century comedy. Their fashions in clothes, their social manners, their tastes in music, art, literature, drink and food is well-documented. Much of the fun in creating one of these characters is the trip you will take into the midst of the period style of their lives.

For convenience, let us refer to the new comedies of the twentieth century merely as comedies. Most of twentieth century comedy is social satire, not farce. Most prime time television comedy is badly written social satire, badly acted in a forced farce technique. The characters in good twentieth century comedies are multidimensional human beings. These comedies always end happily and they look at life from a humorous point of view, but these satirical plays are often about serious subjects and their characters should be allowed to have their serious moments. Careful actors' work must be done on the period style of their lives. They should be brought alive as people, not as comedians or cartoons of people.

Best Comedies Written in the Twentieth Century and Taking Place in the Twentieth Century

Allan Aychborn's *Absurd Person Singular* and *Time and Time Again*
Philip Barry's *Holiday, Philadelphia Story* and *The Animal Kingdom*
Ed Bullins' *The Taking of Miss Janie*
Abe Burrows' *Cactus Flower*
Paddy Chayevsky's *Marty*
Anton Chekhov's *The Sea Gull, Uncle Vanya, The Cherry Orchard* and *The Three Sisters*
Caryl Churchill's *Cloud Nine*
Martin Crowley's *The Boys in the Band*
Bill Davis' *Mass Appeal*
Shelagh Delaney's *A Taste of Honey*
T. S. Eliot's *The Cocktail Party* and *Family Reunion*
Jules Feiffer's *Little Murders*
Herb Gardner's *A Thousand Clowns* and *I'm Not Rappaport*
Leonard Gershe's *Butterflies Are Free* and *Snacks*
William Gibson's *Two for the Seesaw*
Lillian Hellman's *Another Part of the Forest*
Jack Heifner's *Vanities*
Beth Henley's *Crimes of the Heart* and *The Lucky Spot*
Hugh Herbert's *The Moon Is Blue*
Sidney Howard's *They Knew What They Wanted*
Albert Inuarto's *Gemini*

George Kaufman's and Moss Hart's *Once in a Lifetime, You Can't Take It with You, The Man Who Came to Dinner*; Kaufman's and Marc Connelly's *Beggar on Horseback*

Arthur Kopit's *Oh Dad Poor Dad Mama's Hung You in the Closet and I'm Feeling So Sad* (a Dark Comedy)

Allan J. Lerner's *Who Is Harriet Kellerman and Why Is She Looking at Me That Way?*

David Mamet's *Sexual Perversity in Chicago*

W. Somerset Maughm's *The Circle*

Terence McNally's *Frankie and Johnny in the Clair de Lune*

Ferenc Molnar's *The Guardsman*

Richard Nash's *The Rainmaker*

Joe Orton's *Entertaining Mr. Sloan* (a Dark Comedy)

Robert Randall's *Six Rooms Riverview*

David Rimmer's *Album*

George Bernard Shaw's *Pygmalion* and *Major Barbara*

Robert Sherwood's *Reunion in Vienna*

Neil Simon's *The Odd Couple, Plaza Suite, Barefoot in the Park, Come Blow Your Horn, The Star Spangled Girl, Last of the Red Hot Lovers, Promises Promises, California Suite, Chapter Two, Little Me, The Prisoner of Second Avenue, The Gingerbread Lady, Brighton Beach Memoirs, Biloxi Blues, Broadway Bound* and *Rumors*

Bernard Slade's *Same Time Next Year*

Ted Talley's *Hooters*

Kevin Wade's *Key Exchange*

Wendy Wasserstein's *Uncommon Women and Others*

Michael Weller's *Moonchildren* and *Loose Ends*

Twentieth Century Realistic, Sentimental Plays

I have left some fine plays off the comedy and tragicomedy lists because they take neither a generally lighthearted or a generally serious point of view about life. They constantly counterbalance lightheartedness with seriousness. I think of these plays as sentimental plays:

Clifford Odets' *Golden Boy* and *Awake and Sing*

William Saroyan's *My Heart's in the Highlands* and *The Time of Your Life*

Thornton Wilder's *Our Town*

Lanford Wilson's *The 5th of July, Talley's Folly, Talley and Son,* and *The Mound Builders*

Surreal Plays — The mood of these plays is often dream-like or nightmarish, distorted or grotesque. (Actors left to right: Leif Ericson, Anna Niemela, Helen Hayes and author Carlton Colyer. <u>The Skin of Our Teeth</u> by Thornton Wilder, U.S. State Department Tour of South America.)

THE NONREALISTIC, SURREAL, AND ABSURD

There are many plays written in the twentieth century that are a reaction to the predominantly realistic form of most of the plays of the period. These plays are usually about nonrealistic or surreal events. The mood of these plays is often dream-like or nightmarish, distorted or grotesque. They are often timeless and placeless plays. There is always something strange or unworldly or unreasonable about the characters and their behavior. Many of the plays have expressionistic or symbolic elements about them.

There is an historical precedent for these plays: the satyr plays given before tragedies in classical Greece, the seventeenth century Spanish Calderon's *Life Is a Dream,* Shakespeare's plays commonly referred to as romances, *The Tempest, The Winter's Tale* and *Cymbeline* and his comedy, *Midsummer Night's Dream,* and the symbolist plays of the nineteenth century. For the most part, however, the nonrealistic, surreal or absurd plays of the twentieth century are born out of a sense of the loss of human values and the breakdown of communication between people produced by the horrors of the two World Wars. They are products of Nietzsche's and existential philosophy.

The only plays that I think of as Theatre-of-the-Absurd are the basically humorous nonrealistic plays, the plays that present a ridiculous attitude about the unreasonableness of their characters and the incongruence of their events.

Best Twentieth Century Absurd Plays

Samuel Beckett's *Waiting for Godot* and *Endgame*
John Guare's *The House of Blue Leaves*
Eugene Ionesco's *The Bald Soprano* and *The Rhinoceros*

The plays that take a serious but incongruous or unworldly point of view of man's dilemma I think of as nonrealistic or surreal plays.

Best Twentieth Century Nonrealistic or Surreal Plays

Edward Albee's *Zoo Story*
Leonid Andreyev's *He Who Gets Slapped*
Antonin Artaud's *The Spurt of Blood*
Imama Baraka's (Leroy Jones') *The Dutchman*
S. M. Barrie's *Mary Rose*
Edward Bond's *Saved*
Bertold Brecht's *The Resistable Rise of Arturo Ui, The Caucasian Chalk Circle* and *Baal*

Jean Cocteau's *Orphee* and *Oedipe Roi*

Friedrich Duerenmatt's *The Visit*

Jean Genet's *The Maids, The Screens, The Blacks* and *The Balcony.*

Jean Giradoux's *The Madwoman of Chaillot* and *Amphitryon '38*

David Hare's *Plenty* and *Teeth 'N' Smiles*

George Kaiser's *Gas*

Adrienne Kennedy's *Funnyhouse of a Negro*

Maurice Maeterlink's *The Intruder*

Eugene O'Neill's *The Great God Brown, The Hairy Ape* and *The Emperor Jones*

Harold Pinter's *The Homecoming, Old Times, The Caretaker, The Dumbwaiter* and *The Collection*

Luigi Pirandello's *Six Characters in Search of an Author*

Elmer Rice's *The Adding Machine*

David Ruskin's *Ashes*

George Bernard Shaw's *Back to Methusalah*

Sam Shepherd's *Buried Child*

Tom Stoppard's *Jumpers, Travesties* and *Rosencrantz and Guildenstern Are Dead*

August Strindberg's *The Ghost Sonata* and *A Dream Play*

Jean Paul Sartre's *No Exit* and *The Flies*

Michael Tremblay's *Damne Manon, Sacre Sandra* and *Bonjour La Bonjour*

Claude van Italie's *The Serpent*

Peter Weiss' *Marat Sade*

Franz Werfel's *Goat Song*

Thornton Wilder's *The Skin of Our Teeth*

Tennessee Williams' *Camino Real*

Stanislav Ignacy Witkiewicz's *They* and *The Cuttlefish*

Paul Zindell's *The Effect of Gamma Rays on Man in the Moon Marigolds*

INTRINSIC PLAY FORMS AND MODIFICATION

Playing the Intrinsic Form

Obviously, the dramatic form a playwright gives his play is a representation of the attitude the playwright has taken about the subject matter of his play. Aristophanes' *Lysistrata* takes a farcical attitude about war and Euripides' *The Trojan Women*, which realistically explores the horror and suffering that a war can inflict on the noncombatants, takes a tragic attitude about war. Both plays condemn war but they are very different sorts of plays. The characters in a farce are going to be very different sorts of people than the characters in a tragedy. It should be obvious to you that you must be aware of the intrinsic form of a play because that form will strongly affect your choice of psychological objective for the character you are creating for that play. The form of a play will also affect the through line of intention, the way a character pursues his objective within the time frame of a play.

Changing the Period Style

It has been a fad in the 1970s and '80s for directors to change the period style of plays about the past. For some time, staging a play in the period style in which the play was originally conceived has been considered uncreative. Often these creative restagings have resulted in incongruous and confusing productions. Shakespeare's play, *Titus Andronious*, is a bloody, horror-filled melodrama set in the degenerate late Roman Empire. When I saw a production with the characters dressed as 1980s punks and one of the villains with spiked purple hair, it didn't make sense to me. Sometimes, however, plays are updated and put in a modern setting that complements the original period style of the play. The musical *West Side Story* is an updating and a rewriting of Shakespeare's *Romeo and Juliet*. Instead of Renaissance Verona, Italy, the musical is set in modern New York City. The feuding Montague and Capulet families are changed to warring street gangs. I believe that, even if Shakespeare's words had been used in *West Side Story*, the story would have been as available to modern audiences as it has been with Shakespeare's words rewritten. *West Side Story* changes the period style of Shakespeare's play but it maintains the form, spirit, and power of Shakespeare's original tragicomedy.

Producers Have Forced a Form on a Play Without Success

Forcing of a form on a play that the playwright never intended will rarely ever succeed. Here are some specific examples of the mistake made when the intrinsic form of a play is denied: when Samual Beckett's Theatre-of-the-Absurd play, *Waiting for Godot*, was first done on Broadway, Bert Lahr, the comedian, played Estragon as if he were a character in an old comedy farce. This exaggerated impersonation pulled the play out of shape and left it without the haunting, lost, searching quality it should have. The rumor has it that Beckett was disappointed.

Eugene Ionesco was not pleased when the actor Zero Mostel made a farce out of Ionesco's absurd but semiserious, grotesque play, *The Rhinoceros*. Chekhov never forgave Stanislavsky for directing his social comedies as if they were dark and serious tragicomedies.

To this day, the humor and lighthearted attitude about life of Chekhov's characters is lost in heavy-handed you-must-take-all-of-this-seriously productions. The only full-length play of Chekhov's that I consider a tragicomedy is *Ivanov* at the end of which Ivanov shoots himself. The other plays have semisad, seminostalgic endings but it is my belief that Chekhov was not mourning the passing of the period of Russian history about which he was writing; he was saying goodbye to a time in the lives of the upper-middle class of Russia that was charming and frivolous but better off as part of the past than it was a hope for the future.

PSYCHOLOGICAL OBJECTIVE AND THROUGH LINE OF INTENTION

Your research of period style, the exposition given by the playwright, the background material given in the dialogue and descriptive italics, what your character does and says in the time period of the script, plus your consideration of the form in which the script is written should now all come together to breathe life into your character. Once the evidence is all in, the right choice of psychological objective and through line of intention will be the spark of life you need to bring your character alive in a scene and ultimately in the whole play. I believe this choice can be a simple one. Considering all the evidence, is your character a celebrator or a struggler with life?

For me a character's psychological objective is a variation of one of the two basic destinies of human beings. Whether it is a phenomenon that is inherited or whether it is a phenomenon conditioned by a person's early experiences in life from childhood on, people seem destined to either celebrate life or struggle with life.

Strugglers are usually serious people. They may enjoy struggling, but, more often than not, they are slaves to the work they do. They are often very successful, powerful and rich but they often suffer from nervous tension. They constantly feel the need to relax before they go on with their struggle.

Celebrators have a lighthearted attitude about life. They have the capacity to enjoy life for what it is and not for what they make it. Of course, if their celebrating runs away with them, they can celebrate themselves into an early grave.

There are times, of course, when strugglers celebrate and celebrators struggle. Strugglers will celebrate life for a time but, before long, a new challenge to take up the struggle again will present itself and the celebration is over. Strugglers enjoy celebrating the most when they are winning or just after they have won a struggle.

Celebrators may struggle for a time, but, before they realize it, the struggle has turned into a celebration. The work they are doing turns out to be a fun thing to do. If, however, something more fun to do comes along, the previous work may be left undone.

Often, strugglers try to turn themselves into celebrators and vice versa. When you first meet someone, he may seem to be the opposite of what he actually is. On close acquaintance, however, it becomes obvious that a struggler's celebrations are but an aspect of his struggle with life and a celebrator's struggles are but an aspect of his celebration of life.

Unless something cataclysmic or extraordinary happens, a person's destiny to either struggle with life or to celebrate life is a lifetime affair. For your purposes, if you reduce your character's psychological objective in life to a form of struggling or celebrating, you can quickly decide what drives him to do the things he does within the time frame of the play. You can build your character's role within the play and give him a clear through line of intention.

Balancing Intentions with Obstacles

Rehearsing or playing a role is a matter of continually balancing your character's through line of intention with the size or importance of the obstacles to that intention with the amount of energy used to overcome those obstacles. What you do to fulfill your character's through line of intention and how and why you do what you do will be conditioned by what you have realized in your research about your character's style of life. You must keep in mind, however, that the balancing act will also be conditioned by the dramatic form of the play on which you are working.

Changing the Balance of Your Balancing Act to Fit the Dramatic Action of a Play

Not only must your balancing act fit the style of life of your character and the dramatic form of the play, it must also be an act that can change its balance to fit the demands of the dramatic action and structure of the play. As the play progresses towards its happy, sad or tragic ending, the balancing act of the main character or characters must become more and more suspenseful and engrossing to the audience.

Will the hero's energy fail or gain in strength? Will the obstacles to the main character's struggles or celebrations become larger and larger or will they diminish in size and importance? Will your character continue to struggle with life or to celebrate life or will he be overcome by life or the antagonist or the villain in the play?

In each of the acts of a play, will your character overcome one obstacle, relax and then immediately be presented with another obstacle? This is the pattern or structure of the action of a well-made play.

A director will tell you to pick up or slow down the pace or rhythm of your performance but you must learn to think as an actor. You must decide when and where to increase or decrease the size or importance of obstacles and when and where to increase or decrease the energy of your struggle with life or your celebration of life. Only experience will teach you how to change the balance of your balancing act to fit the progress of the dramatic action of a play.

TRAGIC ROLES

Most of the characters in classic tragedies are strugglers with life. At first they may seem to be celebrators of life. They may have moments of celebrating life but, for the most part, they take life seriously.

Villains or Antagonists in Tragedy

Only villains or antagonists such as Iago in Shakespeare's *Othello* or Uncle Ben, the conveyor of false hopes, in Miller's *Death of a Salesman,* can be celebrators of life, but what they celebrate is the dark side of life. They usually present the obstacles to life that will help bring on the tragic downfall of the main character or characters. The more they enjoy their evil deeds, the more the audience is alienated by their behavior; and that's as it should be.

Supporting Characters in Tragedy

If the supporting characters in a classic tragedy become over eager celebrators of the bright side of life, they may create comic interludes that will disrupt the steadily progressing through line of the tragic action.

Aristotle says that, in a classic tragedy, everything should direct the audience's attention toward the impending tragedy. Shakespeare broke Aristotle's rules when he wanted to break them. He created his own form of tragedy. He used farcical, comic interludes such as the Gatekeeper scene in *Macbeth* and the Gravediggers scene in *Hamlet* to break the tension of the tragic struggle in those plays. Shakespeare, however, also wrote pure classic tragedies without any comic interludes — for instance, *Othello* and *King Lear.*

When a playwright has obviously written in the pure tragic form, an actor must not take it upon himself to break that form. Actors should follow the intrinsic form of a playwright's work. Shakespeare can break Aristotle's rules, but an actor must not break the rules a playwright lays down by writing in the dramatic form in which he chooses to write. When there are fun moments to be played in pure tragedy they must not be played as if they were pure comedy.

When Desdemona in Shakespeare's *Othello* quips with Iago about drinking and sex, there must be a sense of the innocent woman striving to prove she is worldly enough to deserve to be the wife of a great general. When Biff and Hap in *Death of a Salesman* joke about Betsy Something with the collie dog, there must be a sense that the joy of youth is lost forever. When Jamie and Edmund in Eugene O'Neill's *Long Day's Journey Into Night* tease and laugh at their father, there must be a sense that this is part of their struggle to get out from under their father's dominance of their lives. On the other hand, if the supporting characters in a tragedy struggle too hard with life they will distract from the main action of the play, the tragic struggle of the main character or characters.

The Main Characters in Tragedy

The main characters in a classic tragedy must not only maintain a serious attitude about life, they must also be careful about the degree of energy they put into their struggling. Usually, the degree of energy a main character puts into his struggle diminishes as the play progresses, and the obstacles to that struggle grow in size or importance.

In the beginning of *Death of a Salesman,* when Willy Loman thinks he may be seen by his wife, he must struggle to carry his heavy sample cases as if he had the strength of a young man. Later in the play, on the other hand, if Willy gets too angry with his neighbor, Charlie, and tries to throw him bodily out of the house, the audience will begin to lose sympathy for Willy's struggle. Still later in the play, if Willy, after he has been told that he has been fired from his job, were to try to smash the tape recorder that is taunting him with the seemingly endless recitation by his boss' son of the capitals of the states, the audience would be confused by the strength of Willy's behavior. If he tries clumsily and hopelessly to find the right button to push and he can barely find the breath to call for his boss to come and help, the audience will sympathize with him. They will realize that he has become a tired old man about to be crushed by the ever-increasing pressures of an uncaring society.

The audience should be aware of the ever-diminishing energy of Willy's struggle but they should also be aware that whenever Willy attempts to celebrate life, he puts too much energy into the attempt. If he brags too hard about his sons or lies too boisterously

Farcical characters are parodies of types of people; therefore you must find someone who is typical of his type. (Miracle play, <u>Noah and His Sons</u>, Dwight Englewood School, Englewood, New Jersey.)

about the amount of the commissions he has made, the audience will be that much more painfully aware of the weakness in Willy's character.

FARCICAL ROLES

The best way to build farcical roles is to study people who remind you of your character. Farcical characters are parodies of types of people; therefore, you must find someone who is typical of his type. Isolate the peculiarities of his physical behavior, physical mannerisms and vocal and facial expressions. Study them but don't mimic them. Let them become part of your sensory image of your character. Let them become organic to the way your character expresses himself. Then, exaggerate them in your building of a ridiculous but essentially human character.

If you can't free yourself to exaggerate the behavior of a farcical character, then use one or more of the "As Ifs" suggested in the Building a Role section. "As Ifs" will help you to exaggerate or to free your behavior and turn it into farcical behavior.

Study Related Disciplines

Farce demands more physical interpretation than any other dramatic form. To be proficient at doing farce, you should take stage combat, juggling, gymnastics, dance, singing and pantomime courses. Use these forms of dramatic expression to free your body and your face and your voice to express themselves as fully as possible. Don't use pantomime to tell the audience what your character is thinking and feeling. Use it, as you did the Clown Faces Exercise, to free your face and body to express themselves more fully than they would in everyday life.

Serious-Minded Farce Characters

The serious-minded strugglers with life are as essential to farce as are the comic celebrators of life. What is funny about the strugglers is that they make mountainous obstacles out of what are actually molehills. The beetle-browed, angry giant of a man who pursues the Little Tramp in Charlie Chaplin movies is funny because he struggles too hard. The obstacles to his struggle, the Little Tramp's agility and the giant's own doltishness and clumsiness, become too much for him and the momentum of the energy he uses to overcome these obstacles brings him crashing to his knees.

Charlie Chaplin, the Consummate Actor of Farce

Charlie Chaplin's work as the Little Tramp is the best of what farcical acting of the comic character can be. Chaplin never stepped out of character to tell us he was being funny. He never tried to force us to laugh.

The Little Tramp is more than just fun. He is a celebrator of life. He is beguiling and sympathetic. He celebrates life with all his senses. Watch his nostrils flare with what smells good or bad, his eyes follow a pretty girl, his fingers reach with a tender touch through the holes in his gloves, and his ears prick up as they sense pleasure or danger. Who else could have turned eating a boiled shoe and its laces into a tasty thrill?

The greatest obstacle to the Little Tramp's celebration of life is the fact that he is little and vulnerable, but he is also quick and agile. He never deigns to put too much energy into his overcoming of an obstacle. He steps aside and watches the charging, beetle-browed giant crash into a heap. At the mercy of a conveyor belt in a pie factory, he lets the pies pile up until they tumble off the assembly line. Then, he twitches his moustache, twirls his cane and waddles off, bemused with the pleasure of it all. We celebrate along with him the triumph of the little man over the seemingly endless obstacles presented to us by a merciless world.

NONREALISTIC, SURREAL OR ABSURD ROLES

They Are Not Farcical Characters

Absurd plays take the attitude that man's dilemma is a ridiculous situation but the characters in absurd plays are all strugglers with life rather than comic celebrators of life. They never struggle too hard with life because life is too much for them. They often try to make fun of their situation but their through line of intention is a serious matter. There is always something sad or pathetic in the ridiculous things they do. Estragon in *Waiting for Godot* struggles to pull his boots off, not to make the audience laugh but because his feet hurt. The boots stick to his feet because the boots are too small and his feet are sweaty. If he struggles too hard to pull off his boots, it is because he is desperate to get them off. The audience may laugh at his contortions but that is a case of humor based on man's inhumanity to man. The audience is saying to themselves, "Thank God I don't have to go through that every night when I take my shoes off." Their laughter is provoked by a sense of their own self-consciousness and relief about the fact that there but for the grace of God, go I.

The Strange, the Grotesque, the Incongruous or the Unworldly

John Guare, who wrote the Theatre-of-the-Absurd play *The House of Blue Leaves,* told me that he never wrote about anybody that he hadn't met. Be that as it may, many of the characters in his plays are not the sort of people I meet every day. The truth in what John Guare told me is that there must be something human as well as incongruous or strange in all of the grotesque or unworldly characters in the best of the nonrealistic, surreal or absurd plays, or we wouldn't care about these characters as much as we do. These plays are often concerned with truths about human existence that we don't want to admit to ourselves.

The best advice I have about building strange, grotesque or unworldly roles is to first find the human elements in the characters and then to distort the character's behavior and thoughts and feelings. Search through the sense-memories of your own unusual or incongruous behavior; study eccentric people; use the "As Ifs" in the Building a Role section and remember your own nightmares.

An Erratic Balancing Act

One of the secrets to building any eccentric role and to freeing yourself to behave strangely or grotesquely is an erratic balancing of your character's intention with obstacle and with energy. Harold Pinter's characters, for instance, sometimes seem to be struggling with too much energy with some unknown obstacle. At other times, the obstacles to their lives seem insurmountable but the characters seem to be doing very little to overcome those obstacles. Their lack or abundance of energy seems inexplicable. Suddenly, without warning, a Pinter character who has seemed without energy or emotion may burst forth with amazing drive and emotion.

The Event, the Atmosphere or the Setting

Often what is nonrealistic or surreal or absurd about these plays is not so much the characters as it is the events, the atmosphere and the setting of the play. There is a mysterious, dream-like or nightmarish quality about it all. The secret then is to make your character as believably human as possible and then let him live as best as he can within the strange world of the play.

Use Your Creative Imagination

Pinter tells you very little about who his characters are or where they are or when the play takes place. He only gives you hints. In *Old Times* he is purposefully indefinite about all the 4 W's. The audience watching this play will never be sure about the relationship of one of the characters to the other two characters. Pinter wants the audience to go away wondering and questioning and trying to find answers. The play will stay with them longer that way.

The actors, however, must justify all of the behavior of their characters. As weird or incongruous as the situation, the characters, the events, the atmosphere, and the setting may be in a nonreal, surreal, or absurd play, you as your character must discover who you are, where you are, when the action takes place, and what you are doing. In the face of all this vagueness, ambiguity and incongruity, you must use your imagination not only to build your character but also to build an exposition for the play and to bring alive the strange world in which you live in the play. It is not your job to make the surreal real or to make sense of the senseless. You, as your character, however, must make the surreal specific. You can't play that of which your senses are unaware. You may have to use sense-memories of your dreams and nightmares. You may have to become sensorially aware as if you were a child or an animal or a drunk or a psychotic.

COMEDY, TRAGICOMEDY AND MELODRAMA ROLES

These are the forms of theatre that give the most latitude to the creation of believable, multidimensional human beings. The characters in comedy can have their serious moments and the characters in tragicomedy can have their humorous moments. In fact, it is the task of the actor to see to it that the character expresses as many aspects of his personality as possible.

Tragicomedy

If the ultimate intent of the script is the presentation of a serious matter, then comedy must not distract from the seriousness of purpose of the through line of action. Humorous, fun moments in tragicomedies can, however, give emphasis and support to the overall seriousness of purpose of the play.

Lessons Learned from Directing Euripides' Iphigenia in Tauris
When I directed Euripides' melodramatic tragicomedy *Iphigenia in Tauris,* I made the mistake of allowing the comic element of the story to outweigh the intrinsic serious action of the play. At times the strugglers struggled too hard and the celebrators

Humorous, fun moments in tragicomedies can give emphasis and support to the overall seriousness of the purpose of the play.(Iphigenia In Tauris, Syracuse University Drama Department.)

celebrated to the point of abandon.

Members of the priestess chorus flirted outrageously with the handsome Greek warriors who were in jeopardy of being sacrificed to Artemis, the goddess the priestesses served. King Taos, the barbaric villain, made too much of his blundering and stumbling and his ranting and raving. Athena, the deus ex machina, who saves the warriors from the wrath of Taos and brings justice and mercy to the laws of man, was more a comedic figure than she was the serious but somewhat vain and satirical personification of common sense as she should be. She used her godly power to get laughs by making Taos a bigger fool than he had made himself. Euripides had written humorous moments into his play and I had encouraged the actors to turn them into farcical moments by overplaying them. The audience loved these farcical touches but I had upset the delicate balance of the comic elements and the serious purpose of the play's through line of action.

On the other hand, the scene in which Iphigenia and Orestes discover that they are each other's long lost brother and sister had just the right degree of fun and humor about it. It supported the melodramatic through line of action. Without their happy reunion, the fact that Iphigenia, the high priestess, might have to sacrifice her own brother would not have been as suspenseful and horrible a prospect as it was. If the other light moments in the script had been done with the same subtlety, they too would have better served Euripides' purposes. The right proportion of fun, comedy and humor is very important to tragicomedy.

Comedy

The actor's first task in creating characters in comedies is to make those characters believable human beings. Neil Simon's first comedies are a series of humorous events and funny lines. If actors don't bring the characters in plays like these alive, the comedy doesn't come alive. Actors playing roles in comedy must allow the serious, vulnerable aspects of their characters to come to the surface. The comic events and funny lines must be connected to the characters' intentions, inner sense-memories or physicalizations. Then the actors will be creating human beings with whom the audience will identify, not one-dimensional comedians whose only intention is to manipulate the audience into laughing.

Comedy Is Not Farce

Comedy, or what was called new comedy and is now often called straight comedy, is a form of social satire or comedy of manners. It is a portrait of a humorous style of life led by a specific group of people at a specific time in human history. This style of life is humorous to others but not to the people living it. These people aren't trying to be funny; they are just living their lives.

Farce paraodies the life and behavior of character types. Actors of farce purposely exaggerate the humorous aspects of their characters. They make as much fun out of their behavior as possible.

If the actors doing straight comedy constantly exaggerate and make fun of what is humorous about their characters, they are playing farce, not comedy. On the other hand, when actors create straight comedy characters, they must realize what is funny about what the playwright has the characters say and do. Actors of comedy must research the period style of the comedy and add what is funny about the thoughts, behavior and manners of the people of that period to the words and events the playwright has created. When actors are playing a comedy role, they must allow their characters to be funny but they must not make fun of their characters or exaggerate what is funny about them.

Overplaying or Underplaying

In old-fashioned terms it was a matter of overplaying farce and underplaying comedy. Both overplaying and underplaying were attempts to manipulate the audience and to let them know when to laugh. The terms had nothing to do with the concentrations and intentions of the character. I suggest that, when playing any role and fitting that role into the dramatic form in which it belongs, it is always a matter of balancing the intention with the size or importance of the obstacles to that intention with the energy used in trying to overcome those obstacles.

It is fun to watch the characters in straight comedy struggle with life and celebrate life in the erratic patterns of actual life. Straight comedy is a portrait of actual life, and, in actual life, people sometimes struggle too hard and it is sad. At other times, they struggle too hard and it is funny. In straight comedy the actors must allow their characters to struggle and to celebrate as the action of the play dictates, but they must be careful not to let the act of balancing intention with object and with energy get out of hand. Playing the sad or serious moments in their characters' lives will bring their characters dimensionally alive but the sad moments should complement the humorous through line of action and not interrupt it. The funny moments in their characters' lives should not be overexaggerated because that will turn the comedy into a farce and the characters into comedians.

Playing Roles in Melodrama

Melodrama became the most popular dramatic form of the last half of the nineteenth century and the beginning of the twentieth century. For the most part melodramatic tragicomedies written during that time are plays of action and suspense. The characters are one-dimensional. The heroes or the good guys struggle against seemingly insurmountable odds. The villains or the bad guys put obstacles in the way of the struggling heroes and then they celebrate the evil deeds they have done. The through line of action is kept going by the fact that, as soon as the hero has overcome one obstacle, another insurmountable obstacle is there and the struggle is on again. The unrelenting pressure of the suspenseful plot is sometimes relieved by incidental moments of comic relief. These moments usually involve either silly or charming characters who innocently celebrate life or who do sentimental things too good to be true.

Productions of nineteenth and early twentieth century melo-dramas developed their own theatrical mode and style of acting. Piano or small orchestra background music emphasized the sus-penseful moments and kept the relentless pressure of the action going. The harder the heroes struggled, the more they won the admiration of the audience and the more the villains celebrated their evil deeds, the more they won the displeasure of the audience.

The melodramatic acting style of the nineteenth and early twentieth centuries was for the most part very broad, obvious and mechanical. Because they played the roles of either the good guy or the bad guy, the sentimental or the silly, there seemed to be no reason for actors to attempt to create multidimensional characters.

Playing "Uncle Tom's Cabin" in the 1960s

When I acted in a production of Harriet Beecher Stowe's famous melodrama *Uncle Tom's Cabin,* the cast decided in rehearsal to try to make the characters as believably human as possible. In performance it seemed as though the more believably human our characters were, the more the audience believed in the dramatic situation. They cheered the exploits of the heroes and hissed the evil deeds of the villains as if the lives of the characters depended on the amount of support or disapproval given them. This, however, was an audience that had been conditioned by acting styles that had evolved as the twentieth century progressed.

STYLES OF ACTING

The Evolution of Acting Styles

There are melodramas that depend as much on multiple di-mensions of character as they do on action and suspense and these were the melodramas that were sought after by the finest of the nineteenth and early twentieth century actors. Henry Irving's most famous melodramatic role was Mathias in Leopold Lewis' *The Bells.* Mathias commits a murder which is undetected and he becomes a successful man as a consequence of it. Gradually, however, Mathias' feelings of guilt get the best of him and he drives himself insane. To our tastes Irving's acting of the role may have been broad and sometimes overdone but he also made Mathias a believable, sympathetic human being.

Turn of the Century Acting Styles

At the turn of the twentieth century the believable human acting of Irving was the exception to the rule. The acting in run-of-the-mill melodramas was broad, one-dimensional and mechanical. The melodramatic style of overacting, however, was not the only style of acting that was prevalent in the late nineteenth and early twentieth centuries. As in the romantic tradition of the early nineteenth century, some actors overemphasized the emotional truth of their characters. Other actors, in the grand manner of most of the international star actors and actresses, ranted and raved, overacted and showed off the splendor of their voices and the uniqueness of their physical gestures.

The Mechanical, Demonstrational Tradition

The idea that acting was a mechanical, demonstrational process used to manipulate audience response didn't want to die. For centuries actors had been trained to find the most dramatic effects in the behavior of their characters. Roles in plays were called lines of business. These lines of business were handed down from one actor to the next. The audience expected an actor to use the same gestures and poses and inflections of voice in performing a role that every other actor had used in playing that role.

The Delsarte System

The most popular actors' training technique of the early twentieth century was the Francois Delsarte System, which taught specific physical gestures and facial expressions that were to be used to express specific human emotions to the audience. Steele MacKaye brought the Delsarte System from France to the United States and it was still being taught in the 1950s when I began acting.

A New Style of Acting Needed

The mechanical, theatrical style of acting, however, was not going to fit the demands of the new dramatic form that was developing at the turn of the twentieth century. In Europe and the United States industrialization had produced a huge, urban working class that was at the mercy of the society in which they lived and worked. Naturalistic plays had begun to take a slice-of-life look at the sometimes sordid lives of these people. The turn of the century plays of Henric Ibsen, George Bernard Shaw and Anton Chekhov realistically portray middle-class characters of the time in the midst of their everyday lives. The characters in these realistic and naturalistic plays are interesting because they are written as believable, multidimensional human beings. They don't lead the theatrically exciting lives of the characters in melodrama, the romantic plays and Shakespeare rewritten to appeal to romantic, sentimental Victorian tastes. That was the theatre that had dominated the stage in the nineteenth century. A new theatre was slowly coming to life.

Creating Multidimensional, Human Characters Not a New Idea

Where did the new acting style for the new theatre come from? The idea of not demonstrating or playing to an audience a character's thoughts and feelings but instead creating a multidimensional, fully human character and allowing that character to exist in a dramatic situation of which the audience was a part was not a new idea.

It is taken for granted that in Shakespeare's *Hamlet,* Hamlet speaks for Shakespeare when he advises the actors about their work in the play within the play. These actors are about to do a play that may shock Hamlet's uncle into revealing his guilt in killing Hamlet's father. Hamlet advises the actors not to overact, not to try to manipulate the audience and not to move and speak as actors but as human beings. Hamlet says, "Suit the action to the word, the word to the action . . ." I interpret this to mean that words written by a playwright should be connected to human behavior, the intentions and actions of a human being.

The Actors Who Took Some of Shakespeare's Advice

We don't know to what extent the actors in Shakespeare's company took Shakespeare's advice, but we do know that Shakespeare wrote dialogue that is best spoken by multidimensional human characters. When Shakespeare's characters are interpreted as human beings and not as theatrical roles, they come alive more fully than perhaps any other characters ever written.

Since the time of Shakespeare, individual actors, in every period of English and American theatre, have attempted to take Shakespeare's advice to heart. Thomas Betterton in the seventeenth century, David Garrick and Charles Macklin in the eighteenth century, and William Charles MacCready, George Frederick Cooke, Edwin Booth and Henry Irving in the nineteenth century were all written about as creating characters that were more believably human than the characters created by other actors of their times. When I read the criticism, contemporary to their times, of their work, I find that these actors did divorce themselves from what was bombastic and overdone in the styles of acting of their times. None of these actors was known for the oratorical delivery of his lines, for bellowing and ranting and raving or for using exaggerated or mechanical gestures or for overplaying emotions. They all took Shakespeare's advice to the extent that they tried to create believably human characters.

Was Henry Irving the First Representational Actor?

When Henry Irving played Shakespeare's Hamlet in 1874, he allowed the character he had created to represent the role Shakespeare had conceived. He did not play his role theatrically; he was satisfied to bring Hamlet alive in front of the audience's eyes.

His Hamlet lived within himself. His soliloquies were spoken not to the audience but to himself.

What is important about Irving's Hamlet is not that he spoke the soliloquies to himself but that he did not feel the obligation to show the audience how Hamlet was thinking and feeling.

Clement Scott, a theatre critic contemporary to Irving, wrote, "We in the audience see the mind of Hamlet . . . .Mr. Irving intended to conjure up the features of the king by . . . seeing them with his mind's eye only." Irving used his creative sense-memories to bring alive the mental images that resulted in Hamlet's believably human vocal and facial expression. He did not make faces at the audience or use mechanical vocal inflections to indicate to the audience the depth of Hamlet's feelings. Irving's Hamlet may have been the first nondemonstrational, honest portrayal of a believable human character.

A New Style of Acting

Constantin Stanislavsky built a technique or system of acting on the premise that, without demonstrating their characters' thoughts and feelings, multidimensional human characters can exist in a dramatic situation of which the audience is a part. If a character is a believable human being, individual human beings in the audience will share the thoughts and feelings of that character and respond to them as one human being to another.

Stanislavsky's system has grown and adapted itself into a style of acting that is the essence of all of the fine acting of today. This new style may have been inspired by the naturalistic and realistic plays of the turn of the century but it was anticipated by Shakespeare and actors like Henry Irving and others before him. This writer believes that the style or technique of acting that has evolved out of Stanislavsky's teaching is the best technique for interpreting all the dramatic forms of theatre of the past, the present and the future.

The Actors Who Could Have Been the Models for the New Style of Acting

Stanislavsky did not conceive his system out of the inspiration of his own genius. He never was or claimed to be a consummate actor. Irving may have been the first but there were other late nineteenth and early twentieth century actors who helped inspire the new style of acting. Stanislavsky conceived his system by studying the rehearsal and performance techniques of Elenora Duse, Thomaso Salvini and Ernesto Rossi of Italy, and Maria Yermolova of the Maly Theatre in Moscow.

Although Stanislavsky did not know their work, it is said that America's William Gillette and Margaret Anglin and England's Ellen Terry, all of whom worked during the same period as the actors who were Stanislavsky's models, had developed an acting style similar to that of the actors that Stanislavsky studied firsthand.

It is not the purpose of this book to present Stanislavsky's system to you. Instead, offered here is information about the best of the work of actors, teachers and directors who have adapted, improved and added to what Stanislavsky originally taught.

Many techniques of acting have been presented over the last eighty years or more that are said to contradict what Stanislavsky taught, for instance, the theories of Antonin Artaud, Vsevold Meyerhold, Bertold Brecht, Jerzy Grotowski and Peter Brook. These theories would contradict Stanislavsky if they based the creation of dramatic characters on something other than multidimensional human beings or if they recommended demonstrational audience manipulation acting. The theories of the teachers listed here don't contradict what Stanislavsky taught; they adapt and try to improve Stanislavsky's work.

Theories of Artaud, Meyerhold, Brecht, Grotowski and Brook

In order to disturb and to provoke an audience into thinking objectively and taking seriously what they are witnessing on the stage, Artaud's theory of a theatre of cruelty advocates the manifestation of nightmares and horrible and shocking events on the stage.

Brecht's epic theatre used music, choral passages and movie-projected images to instruct the audience and to make political or social comments on the dramatic events. He used geste, or the perfect choice of dramatic activity, to wake up an audience's social consciousness. An example of such a geste is to have a character suddenly kick a pregnant woman character in the belly. The pregnant woman screams, clutches her belly, doubles over and runs off the stage. From the other side of the stage a clown appears who mimics and makes fun of the painful gyrations of the pregnant woman who has been kicked in the belly. This geste is also an example of what Brecht called verfrumdung or detachment, an interruption of an audience's subjective involvement in the dramatic event and a provocation of their objectivity about what they are experiencing. No one is going to leave the theatre and forget the moment of the clown and the pregnant woman. They are going to think about the social implications of what they have witnessed.

Brecht asked his actors to be intelligent enough and objective enough in rehearsal, when they were building their roles, to make choices of a character's intention, action and behavior that would make the political or social statement Brecht wanted that character to make. In performance he sometimes had his characters step out of character and speak as the actor directly to the audience. Contrary to what some people believe, he never asked his actors to stand outside of their characters and to make comments about their characters' behavior while those characters were involved in the main dramatic action of the play. The story lines of Brecht's plays always present the events of actual life and they always involve multidimensional human beings. He often hired Stanislavsky-trained actors to play the roles in his plays.

Brook and Grotowski advocate theatre without proscenium arches, traditional sets, costumes and props. They talk of improvisational, moment-to-moment acting and environmental staging.

Grotowski and Meyerhold both talk about working from the outside in rather than the inside out while creating a character. Meyerhold's theory of biomechanics states that a physical experience can provoke inner thoughts and feelings.

The Style of Acting Taught in This Book

Most of what Stanislavsky taught did advocate working from inside out. For him inner sense-memory was the source of physicalization, specific physical states of being and physical activity and action. This book has directed you to work on specific physical states of being, activities and obstacles to invoke inner thoughts and feelings. You have also worked on inner sense-memories and inner monologues to invoke physical, vocal and facial expression. You are learning to work from the inside out and the outside in.

In the "As If" section many ways are suggested for you to bring Artaud-like dreams and nightmares to life. You will learn specific ways of creating unworldly, grotesque characters and incongruous events.

Shakespeare's soliloquies are written for the character to share his thoughts and feelings with individuals in the audience. Stepping out of character and speaking as the actor directly to the audience doesn't contradict what Stanislavsky taught or what is taught here. The audience should be part of the dramatic event, not just a witness to it. We have already talked about audience response being an important part of the actor's performance experience.

You have learned to work without props, sets and costumes. You know how to bring an empty space to life. You have practiced improvisation and immediate, moment-to-moment actors' work. You have a working knowledge of much of what Peter Brook in *The Empty Space,* Antonin Artaud in *The Theatre and Its Double,* Jerzy Grotowski in *Towards a Poor Theatre,* Bertold Brecht in *Brecht on Theatre,* and Vsevold Meyerhold in *Meyerhold on Theatre* have to say. Everything the theorists who reacted or responded to Stanislavsky is not included here for want of space. The student may pursue this at greater length on his own if the subject is intriguing.

What Stanislavsky taught and what the theorists I have talked about have done is to build a new style of acting that makes theatre a believable, human experience, not a theatrical, phony experience. Theatre exists not only to entertain but also to provoke thoughts, feelings and action. If people go to the theatre and learn something about love or they experience anything important about human relationships and they do nothing about what they have learned or experienced, then theatre has failed.

Interpreting Plays with the Style of Acting Used in the Original Production

It is one thing to do a play in the social style of the period of history about which the play is written and in the intrinsic dramatic form of the play. It is another thing to do a play from the past in the style of acting as originally done. It can be of historical interest to interpret a play as originally interpreted, but working in antiquated techniques of acting should be last on your list in learning the fine art of acting.

The plays of Corneille and Racine take on a massive importance when done in the baroque, mannerist, oratorical style of acting of the time when their plays were written and originally produced. The best interpretation I have seen of Racine's *Phedra* was a production in which the actors created multidimensional human beings and let them speak to each other as human beings would speak.

PROGRESSIVE WORK IN SCENE CLASS

Begin by working on two or three expository scenes from a twentieth century tragedy or tragicomedy. The act of balancing intention with obstacles with the energy used to overcome those obstacles is less of a challenge in expository scenes than it would be in emotional or comic scenes. Also, work for a while on characters that are close to you in age and type of personality. Learn first to adapt a role to fit yourself and later you can begin to adapt yourself to fit a role.

Read the whole play and do the following: research the style of life of your character; improvise moments in your character's life that happened before the time frame in which the play takes place; establish a relationship with the people and places in your character's present life; know your character's psychological objective in life and his through line of intention in the play; and establish the 4 W's of the scene and adapt them to your partner's work. You should then be able to easily score your scene with intention, activity and beats of action.

After working on a few expository scenes, it should become an easier task to get the playwright's words to become part of the moment-to-moment life of your character. Before you know it, following your character's intentions beat by beat and playing off the moment-to-moment work of your partner, the 4 W's will overlap by themselves. Without your being continuously aware of each step of the procedure, you will bring a multidimensional character to life in front of an audience.

Scenes of Struggling and Celebrating, Power Playing and Emotional Release

It is best to alternate between creating characters who struggle with life and characters who celebrate life. After doing a few serious expository scenes, do a serious power playing scene that will help you connect the multiple dimensions of a specific role to a dramatically exciting event. Next, pick a scene that calls for power playing and emotional release and see if that emotional release will flow out of the moment-to-moment work you have planned in rehearsal. If you have scored the scene properly and you concentrate on the power play as it happens, you won't anticipate the moment of emotional release. The dramatic climax of the event will be there before you know it, and you can relax and let the emotional moment happen of its own accord.

Scenes of Comedy, Farce, Absurd and the Surreal

Next, do scenes from twentieth century comedies in which the lighthearted mood of the scenes depends on a delicate balance of struggling with life or celebrating life. The size of the obstacles to that struggle or celebration should be balanced with the degree of energy needed to overcome those obstacles. It is the actor's task in building comedy roles to add physical behavior, period manners, and thoughts and feelings to the funny words and comic events the playwright has created. A character's behavior in comedy must enhance the funny lines the playwright has written for that character. It must also reveal the serious aspects of a multidimensional character. Good vocal production is important in all your work but clear articulation and a variety of vocal tone is especially important in comedy. If an audience doesn't understand the funny things you say, not only won't they laugh, but they will get annoyed with you. Free your natural voice and free the joints, muscles and limbs of your body before you do any actor's work in comedy.

After doing straight comedies do a farcical, grotesque or dark comedy scene in which you have to exaggerate specific elements of your character's physical and vocal expression. Remember, the humor in farce is often based on a struggler's making mountains out of molehills and using too much energy to overcome those obstacles. The celebrators, on the other hand, overcome obstacles with grace and agility. Warm up those limbs, joints and muscles.

Doing scenes from absurd plays will challenge your ability to create a specific, multidimensional life for your character, very little of which will be given to you by the playwright.

To create absurd, surreal or farcical characters you may have to free or justify their physical behavior and thought patterns by working as if you were a child, an animal, intoxicated or psychotic. Balancing intention with obstacle and with energy when playing an absurd or surreal character can be an erratic, incongruous, unreasonable experience.

PRE-TWENTIETH CENTURY STYLES

The next step is to work on scenes from plays written before the twentieth century. Use your technique of acting. It will serve you better than the outdated style of acting that might have been originally used to interpret a play from the past.

Learn to build roles with a lifestyle that is very different from yours. Learn about the physical surroundings, the social manners and philosophical outlook of people from many different periods of history. Build roles and create characters whose social stature or position is completely foreign to you. Work with words you don't use every day.

Working in Pre-Twentieth Century Modes

Save working in the original theatrical mode as a final step in your work on period plays but, after you have worked in the world of a specific period of the past as it actually would have been outside the theatre, then have some fun. Research the specific ways plays were staged when they were first produced. As an interesting challenge, work in a facsimile of the actor-to-audience relationships of the past. Try to work in the acting area and with only the props and furniture that were originally used.

Classic Greek and Roman Settings

Work as classical Greek and Roman actors did in an amphitheatre setting with an audience of at least five thousand people three-quarters of the way around and above you. Unless you want to pay five thousand people to watch you, you will, or course, have

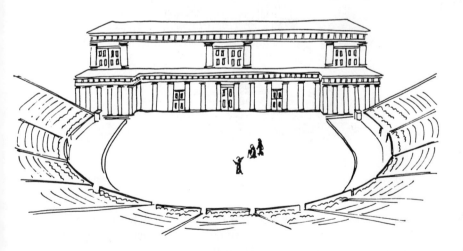

Greek amphitheatre

167

to imagine the amphitheatre's audience. Your acting space is the bare, round flat surface of the orchestra or a thirty-foot-long, five-foot-wide, barely elevated platform that flattens a quarter of the circumference of the orchestra. The platform is backed with the facade of a palace or a temple. Your first entrance and final exit is up or down ramps, one at each end and in front of the long narrow platform. The ramp stage right leads toward the sea. The ramp stage left leads inland.

Sixteenth Through Eighteenth Century Settings

Work as Shakespeare's actors did on a thrust platform stage about five feet high, and about fifteen feet square. About ten members of the audience are sitting on benches or stools along the edges of the stage to your right and left. The rest of the audience of about five hundred people is standing in the pit below and around the stage or is seated in tiers of balconies above and around you. There are very few props and only one or two pieces of furniture and no set. There may be a small alcove surrounded with four posts

thrust stage

at the rear of the stage you can use as an antechamber or a cave. The only exits and entrances are curtained doorways, one on each upstage side of the acting platform.

Work as seventeenth and eighteenth century actors did on a thrust stage with few props and no furniture. You must work standing up. There is an illusionary set of painted flats diminishing in space behind you and the proscenium arch. You as your character may refer or relate to this elaborate setting behind you but you can never move into it. The acting space is the approximately twenty square feet of the thrust stage in front of the proscenium arch. Only the downstage center of this space is well lighted. The only exits and entrances are doors that open offstage, one on either side of the proscenium arch.

Nineteenth Century Settings

Work as if you were in a forty square foot area that is boxed in by realistically painted flats. The boxed-in acting area is behind a huge proscenium arch which you must treat as an imaginary fourth wall. You can talk directly to the audience when you have an aside to speak; otherwise, you must pretend that the audience is not there. The box set has working doors and windows in it. The set is furnished realistically and you can sit on the chairs and benches and lean or perch on the tables or the backs of the chairs or sofas. Be careful, however; some of the furniture is painted on the flats. You can have all the realistic props you need.

box set scene

Activities, Actions, Clothing, Deportment, Speech Social Manners and Dialects

Because they usually told stories about the ruling class, the aristocracy or the upper-middle class, with the exception of the naturalistic plays few pre-twentieth century plays were set in kitchens or workplaces. There were pastoral or outdoor scenes but, for the most part, plays were set in palace courtyards and antechambers or the drawing rooms, sitting rooms or parlors of large houses. When you first work on period plays, work in a twentieth century acting style and theatrical mode. Use the objects and the furniture you need to use to bring the action of a scene alive.

Do your period research. Get acquainted with the art book section of your library. Read novels and biographies about the period of history in which your character lived. Get to know the places and people and things from a specific period in the past involving your charcter. Use the objects that would be in the place where your character is going to come alive.

Physical activity was often dictated by the tightness or looseness of the clothes that were worn. If they wore tights or tight trousers, men liked to show off the shape of a good leg. Women often moved to display or show off the sweep and the flow of their dresses.

Bowing and curtsying were an important part of social behavior but people bowed and curtsied differently at different times in history. In the past, ladies and gentlemen were taught physical deportment and specific styles of dancing that differed greatly from one period to the next. From the Middle Ages to the nineteenth century, men were taught the proper way to fence and to sit on a horse.

In the eighteenth and nineteenth centuries many people suffered from gout. That's one of the reasons why footstools were placed in front of easy chairs. For centuries, unless they were alone, ladies and gentlemen never leaned back in any chair in which they sat. For many centuries, people were severely pockmarked and, therefore, both men and women wore layers of make-up. Only very recently has central heating been installed in English homes. In times past, ladies and gentlemen warmed their hands and their behinds in front of fireplaces. Until late in the nineteenth century there was no indoor plumbing. That's why there were folding screens in almost every room: chamber pots lived behind these screens. There were times when both ladies and gentlemen and their servants wore elaborate wigs and high heels.

All of this had a direct bearing on how men and women moved from one place to another and physically related to each other. Bring your character alive by creating physical activity that is of the period in which your character lived.

The Space Outside the Acting Space

In today's productions of period plays there is often very little in the way of a set. This is the time of abstract scenic design. Even, however, if the stage is bare, you, as your character, must have a specific sensory awareness of where you are, where you have been, and where you may be going. You must geographically physicalize the places, people and events outside your acting area to which the dialogue of the play refers.

Just as in twentieth century plays, the people, places and events referred to by your character should have specific locations toward the audience. Of course, your sense-memories in period plays must be memories of the people and places you have experienced in your research of that period.

Clothing

You can research the style of dress of a period in costume books. Actors may have worked with few props or little or no furniture, but in every period of theatre production no expense was spared on costumes. Performers dressed as they thought their characters would have dressed in actual life. Queen Anne gave Charles II's coronation robes to the great actor Thomas Betterton to wear when he portrayed a king upon the stage. Before you rehearse or even improvise a scene from a period play, put on garments that will substitute for the clothes your character would have worn. Don't rehearse scenes from period plays in jeans and sneakers. Jeans and sneakers have been everyday wear only since the 1970s.

Deportment

Just because you are creating ladies and gentlemen of the past, don't stiffen up as you sit and stand and move. Well-bred people of the past had both common sense and a sense of grace. They knew that physical tension was a sign of social discomfort or self-consciousness. Dancing, fencing and training in physical deportment taught them to walk, sit and stand in alignment. When they were aligned, they knew they presented a relaxed and, at the same time, assured image.

Start from alignment and then vary that alignment to compensate for your character's physical infirmities or specific physical states of being: his weariness, or being chilled or hot. Keep in mind, however, that ladies and gentlemen of the past tried very hard to move with grace and assurance despite how they felt physically or mentally. If they were aware that they were out of alignment, they would bring themselves back into it as best they could.

In the discussion of Psychological Center in the Building a Role section of this book, you will learn that variations of the body's true alignment can express your character's psychological attitude about life. Even in times when physical grace and deportment were a way of life, a person's psychological attitude might distort that person's physical alignment without that person being aware of it. Eccentric characters in period plays won't have the same physical grace that socially well-adjusted characters will have.

Speech

Ladies and gentlemen of the past used language much more carefully, easily and precisely than we do. Even when they weren't speaking out loud they were careful about the language they used. They constantly wrote notes and letters and those notes and letters used polite, formal language. Don't you, however, use phony formal diction or pseudo-English in an attempt to reproduce the way ladies and gentlemen of the past spoke.

Look up the words the playwright uses that aren't familiar to you. Know the exact meaning of what you are saying before you say it. When you speak, standard stage speech will do perfectly well. Relax and enunciate and articulate. Connect what you are saying to what your character is thinking, doing and intending, and the language will take care of itself.

Social Manners

Another name for social satire is Comedy of Manners. In your research you must become acquainted with the social manners of the period no matter in what dramatic form you are working. There are books written specifically about the social manners of different periods.

There were times when a lady would never have been seen in company without her fan. Ladies were taught the language of the fan and this language differed from one period to the next. For centuries, gentlemen never went anywhere without a cane or a sword and gloves and a hat. In the eighteenth century taking snuff was as much a part of polite social behavior as was smoking cigarettes in the first half of the twentieth century.

Dialects

Of course, if you work on a character who speaks English with a foreign accent — in any play, not just period plays — you will have to work on a dialect to fit the character. Tapes of foreign dialects can be purchased through drama bookstores. Only in cases like Oscar Wilde's and Noel Coward's comedies must you use an aristocratic English accent. The characters won't come alive without it. Think of the accent as another foreign dialect. Listen to Noel Coward records or to recordings of nineteenth and twentieth century English poets reading their own poetry. You will soon discover that a good English accent is more a matter of rhythm than it is pronunciation. Irish, Cockney and other English regional dialects are foreign accents to an American ear. All accents can be learned by ear and then practiced while using the playwright's words. A compromise always has to be made between producing a perfect accent and adapting that accent to theatre or movie work. The accent must not prevent the audience's understanding of the meaning of what your character is saying.

Best Pre-Twentieth Century Plays

Here are some plays in which to find good scenes. Challenge yourself. Work in as many periods of style as possible. Create characters older and younger than you are and characters whose personalities are very different from your personality. Play strugglers and celebrators and leading roles and supporting roles. Always create multidimensional human beings but discover if you are the sort of actor who creates characters who resemble yourself more than they do somebody else, or if you are the sort of actor who creates characters who resemble somebody else more than they resemble you. Most actors fit into one category or the other and neither sort of actor is better than the other.

Frequently Performed Pre-Twentieth Century Plays:

GREEK AND ROMAN
Aristophanes' *Lysistrata* and *The Frogs*
Plautus' *The Menaechmi*
Euripides' *Medea* and *The Trojan Women*

SHAKESPEARE
HISTORIES: *Julius Caesar, King Richard III*
COMEDIES: *Twelfth Night, As You Like It* and *Much Ado About Nothing*
TRAGICOMEDIES: *The Merchant of Venice* and *Romeo and Juliet*
TRAGEDIES: *Othello, Hamlet, Macbeth* and *King Lear*
ROMANCES: *The Tempest* and *A Midsummer Night's Dream*
FARCE: *The Taming of the Shrew*

ENGLISH RESTORATION AND LATE EIGHTEENTH CENTURY
SOCIAL SATIRES OR COMEDIES OF MANNERS
William Wycherley's *The Country Wife*
William Congreve's *The Way of the World*
Richard Brindsley Sheridan's *The Rivals* and *The School for Scandal*
Oliver Goldsmith's *She Stoops to Conquer*

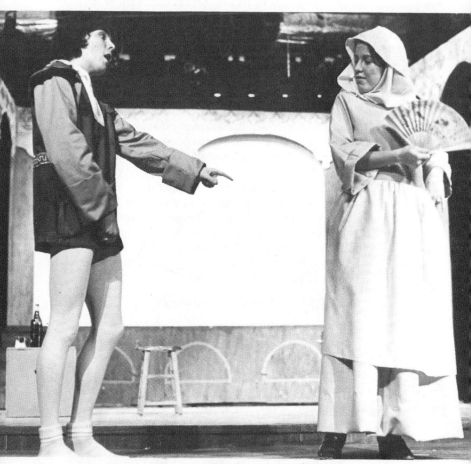

Create characters older and younger than you are and characters whose personalities are very different from your personality. (<u>Romeo and Juliet</u> by William Shakespeare, Dwight Englewood School, Englewood, New Jersey.)

LATE NINETEENTH AND TWENTIETH CENTURY ENGLISH COMEDY
(Because of their special challenge and the language spoken, Noel Coward's plays are included here and not with a list of twentieth century plays.)
> Oscar Wilde's *The Importance of Being Earnest* and *Lady Windemere's Fan*
> Noel Coward's *Fallen Angels, Hay Fever, Bittersweet, Private Lives* and *Design for Living.*

Pre-Twentieth Century Plays that Should Be Done More Often:

GREEK AND ROMAN
FARCE: Aristophanes' *The Birds* and *The Clouds*
> Euripides' *The Cyclops (a satyr play)*
TRAGICOMEDY: Euripides' *Hippolytus, Andromache, Hecuba, Iphigenia in Tauris* and *The Bacchae*
NEW COMEDY: Manander's *The Grouch,* Terence's *The Mother In Law* and *The Eunuch*
FARCE: Plautus' *Amphitryon*

SIXTEENTH CENTURY
FARCE: Flaminio Seala's commedia scenarios
> William Shakespeare's *The Merry Wives of Windsor* and *A Comedy of Errors*
> Pierre Gringore's *The Prince of Fools*
> The Wakefield Master's *Noah and His Sons* and *The Second Shepherd's Play*
> Nicholas Udall's *Ralph Roister Doister*
MORALITY PLAY: *Everyman*
COMEDY OF HUMORS: Ben Jonson's *Volpone, The Alchemist* and *Bartholomew Fair*
HISTORIES: William Shakespeare's *King Richard II, King Henry V* and *King Henry IV (parts 1 and 2)*
TRAGICOMEDY: Niccolo Machiavelli's *The Mandrake*
> William Shakespeare's *Measure for Measure, All's Well That Ends Well* and *Troilus Cressida*
> Torquato Tasso's *Aminta*
> Giambattista Guarini's *The Faithful Shepherd*
SENECAN TRAGEDY: Cinthio's *Obecche, Dido* and *Cleopatra*
> Thomas Kyd's *The Spanish Tragedy*
> Christopher Marlow's *Dr. Faustus* and *Edward III*
TRAGEDIES: William Shakespeare's *Antony and Cleopatra, Timon of Athens* and *Coriolanus*
ROMANCES: William Shakespeare's *Cymbeline* and *The Winters Tale*

SEVENTEENTH CENTURY
TRAGEDY: John Webster's *The White Devil* and *The Duchess of Malfi*
> John Fletcher's and Francis Beaumont's *A King and No King*
TRAGICOMEDY: Miguel de Cervantes' *The Seige of Numancia* and *The Fortunate Ruffian*
> Lope de Vega's *The Sheep Well*
> Pierre Corneillie's *Le Cid*
> Jean Racine's *Phedre*
NON-REALISM: Pedro Calderon's *Life Is a Dream*

HEROIC TRAGEDY: John Dryden's *All for Love*
    Thomas Otway's *Venice Preserved*
FRENCH SOCIAL FARCES:
    Moliere's *Tartuffe, The Misanthrope, The Imaginary Invalid* and
    The School for Wives

EIGHTEENTH CENTURY

COMMON LIFE TRAGEDY: George Lillo's *The London Merchant*
    Ephraim Lessing's *Minna Von Barnhelm*
TRAGEDY: Voltaire's *Zaire*
LAUGHING COMEDY: John Vanbrugh's *The Relapse* and *The Provoked
    Wife*
    Henry Fielding's *Tom Thumb*
SENTIMENTAL FARCES: Carlo Goldoni's *Mirandolina or the Mistress of
    the Inn* and *The Servant of Two Masters*
    Carlo Gozzi's *The Love of Three Oranges* and *The King Stag*
SENTIMENTAL COMEDY: Richard Steele's *The Conscious Lovers*
    Pierre Marivaux's *The Game of Love and Chance*
    Pierre de la Chausse's *False Antipathy* and *The Fashionable
    Prejudice*
    Voltaire's *The Prodigal Son*
LAUGHING COMEDY: Beaumarche's *The Barber of Seville* and *The Mar-
riage of Figaro*

NINETEENTH CENTURY

WEIMAR CLASSICISM: Fredrich Schiller's *The Robbers, Wallenstein's
    Camp, Mary Stuart* and *Don Carlos*
    Goethe's *Faust*
EARLY MELODRANA: August Kotzebue's *The Stranger* and *Pizzaro*
ROMANTIC PLAYS: Ludwig Tieck's *Kaiser Octavianus*
    Henrich von Kleist's *Prince of Homburg*
    Edmond Rostand's *Cyrano de Bergerac*
    Alexandre Dumas pere's *The Three Musketeers*
    Victor Hugo's *Cromwell* and *Hernani*
    George Buchner's *Danton's Death*
    Alexander Pushkin's *Boris Gudonov*
EARLY REALISM: Friedrich Hebbel's *Maria Magdalena*
    Nikolai Gogol's *The Inspector General*
MELODRAMA: Bulwer-Lytton's *Richelieu* and *Money*
    Monk Lewis' *Ambrosio, or the Monk*
    Douglas Jerrold's *Black-Eyed Susan*
    Pierce Egan's *Tom and Jerry or Life in London*
    Baldwin Blackstone's *Luke the Laborer*
    Tom Taylor's *The Ticket of Leave Man*
    T. W. Robertson's *Caste*
    Leopold Lewis' *The Bells*
    Harriet Beecher Stowe's *Uncle Tom's Cabin*
LATER REALISM: Arthur Wing Pinero's *The Second Mrs. Tanqueray*
    Henry Arthur Jones' *The Liars*
    John Galsworthy's *Justice*
WELL-MADE PLAYS: Alexander Dumas fils' *Camille*
    Eugene Scribe's *A Glass of Water*
    Victorien Sardou's *A Scrap of Paper* and *Tosca*

LATER MELODRAMA: Dino Boucicault's *London Assurance* and *The Octoroon*

REALISM: Thomas William Robertson's *Society* and *Caste*
    William Gillette's *Sherlock Holmes* and *The Secret Service*
    Clyde Fitch's *Beau Brummel*
    August Strindberg's *The Father* and *Miss Julie*
    Ivan Turgenev's *A Month in the Country*
    Alexey Tolstoy's *The Death of Ivan, the Terrible*

NATURALISM: Leo Tolstoy's *Power of Darkness*
    Emile Zola's *Therese Raquin*
    Henri Becque's *The Vultures*
    Gerard Hauptman's *The Weavers*

SYMBOLISM, NONREALISM: Oscar Wilde's *Salome*
    Maurice Maeterlink's *Pelleas and Melisande*
    Franz Wedekind's *Spring Awakening, Earth Spirit, Pandora's Box* and *The Tenor*

LATE NINETEENTH CENTURY WELL-MADE PLAYS

COMEDIES: George Bernard Shaw's *Arms and the Man, Candida, Caesar and Cleopatra* and *Mrs. Warren's Profession*

TRAGICOMEDIES: Henrik Ibsen's *A Doll House, Ghosts, An Enemy of the People* and *Hedda Dabler*

When you use physical and psychological centers to help you create a character, let yourself think and feel as you think and feel. (Author Carlton Colyer as Jamie in <u>Long Days Journey Into Night</u> by Eugene O'Neill, Center Stage, Baltimore, Maryland.)

3. BUILDING A ROLE

DEVELOPING A CHARACTER

The exercises in this section may also be used for work in front of a camera.

Did you ever come out of a movie and, without your being conscious of beginning it, you were walking and talking like the hero or heroine in the movie? I think this is a case of half mimicry and half coming alive as a character in a dramatic environment. Many times, when I was a boy, I came out of westerns and my body wanted to move as John Wayne had moved, and it did. I began to react to the real life situation outside the movie house as if I were John Wayne. I was speaking with his tone of voice. I was still involved in the atmosphere and the personal relationships of the movie. All of it had rubbed off on me and affected me psychologically.

What impressed me was not that I was walking and talking like Big John but that I was doing it subconsciously. I usually stopped when I was conscious of what I was doing because I didn't want my friends to think I was trying to do a John Wayne impression.

After you have read a play, realized its dramatic form, selected a character to create, researched the style of life of that character and made decisions about the character's psychological objective in life and through line of intention in the play, you are ready to get that character on his feet and to begin to walk and talk as that character. You haven't seen your character in a movie, but if you relax and close your eyes you can create your own sense-memory experiences of that character.

Exercise: Create Your Own Movie-Like Experience

Lie down on the floor on your back and do a complete physical and mental relaxation exercise. When you are as relaxed as possible, begin to see your character on that sense-memory screen inside your head just above your eyes. If you have researched your character's style of life thoroughly, you ought to begin to see a specific place in which your character might live. Explore that place. See the objects there, the color, shape, size and texture of things. Hear, smell, taste and feel that place.

Now, begin to see your character within that place. Is he sitting or standing? Perhaps your character is in the midst of an activity. Feel, smell, taste and listen to what he is doing. Let your character settle down or come to rest sitting or standing within this specific place.

Realize the size and weight of your character. Look at the color and texture of your character's hair, the shape and size of his head, the color and shape of his eyes, the planes and angles of his face.

What is his complexion? Are your character's face and hands wrinkled, freckled, pockmarked or tanned? What do you like or dislike about your character's physical appearance?

See and feel your character's clothes. Realize the tightness or looseness of those clothes. Feel the weight and texture of what he is wearing. What is on his feet?

Let your character involve himself in an activity again. Be aware of how your character moves. What are his specific states of physical being? Can you begin to feel where he is heavy or thin, weak or strong, tired or exhilarated, warm or cold?

Can you hear your character speak to another person? Listen to the tone, resonance, articulation and projection of his voice.

You have created your own movie-like experience. When you have had a total sensory experience of your character and you get up off your back and on to your feet and you begin to move and behave as that character, much of what your character does and the way he expresses himself will be a subconscious experience, just as it was when I began to talk and behave like John Wayne.

Use of a Video Cassette Recorder

If you have someone in mind who reminds you of the character you are creating, why not get that person's physical behavior and vocal expression on tape? Some people are very shy and self-conscious in front of a camera but, if you can catch your subject at work or in the middle of an involving activity at home, he will be less likely to feel obliged to perform and will behave naturally.

If you tell your subject a joke or a story, maybe he will try to top you and keep on working at the same time. Then, you will get some footage of vocal and physical expression that can help you build some of the dimensions of your character.

The use of tape playback is obvious. If your subject does behave or speak or gesture or move as you think your character would, watching the tape will be like my watching a John Wayne movie. Watch the tape and let your subject's impressions on you incorporate themselves, subconsciously, into your multifaceted image of your character.

Don't Mimic

Don't pause or slow motion the tape as you play it back. Don't consciously try to copy a gesture, a voice inflection or a physical mannerism. That would be like practicing in front of a mirror a specific facial expression to match a specific emotion.

Whether or not you tape them, don't let your studies of a person similar to your character become mechanical mimicry of that person. Let your sense-memories of the people you study blend with the rest of your research of a role. Let the sense-memories of your character incorporate themselves into the total 4 W's image of your character.

Methods of Putting Together Your Images of a Character and Manifesting Him or Her as a Multidimensional Human Being

I believe lying down and relaxing and watching the sense-memory images of your character come together on your inner sense-memory screen should always be one of the final steps in building a role. There are things, however, that you can look for as you study and research that will help you put all of your images of your character together into one person. As you get up and move and behave in character, there are specific ways of checking to see if your character is expressing himself as you feel he should express himself.

PHYSICAL AND PSYCHOLOGICAL CENTERS

While you are studying people similar to your character or you are looking at pictures or movies of people of the past who could be your character, see if you can discover the physical center of balance your character should have. As I have said, socially well-adjusted ladies and gentlemen of the past attempted to maintain alignment at all times. They probably came closer to doing it than the people of today.

The Hip Joint or What?

The physical center of balance for someone who sits, stands and moves in true alignment is that person's hip joints. As your character sits, stands and moves, even if he is a period character, he will be somewhat or perhaps a good deal out of alignment.

If the trunk of your character's body is thrust forward, then the center of balance is the toes. Those toes have to work hard to prevent that person from falling flat on his face. By the way, people who walk and move with the trunk of their body thrust forward (the thrust can be slight or exaggerated) are usually ambitious, go-get-'em strugglers with life. A study of someone's physical center of balance can be very revealing about that person's personality or his psychological objective in life.

Psychological Center

Instead of working from the outside in to discover how someone physically expresses his personality, try working from the inside out. When you have discovered your character's psychological objective in life, think about where it would be natural for his wants or needs in life to be expressed physically. If a woman is celebrating life and she is proud of her breasts, she often lets her chest lead her through life. Her breasts are her psychological center. Her physical center of balance is in both the knees and the small of her back. Try letting a heavy, thrust-forward chest lead you around a room. Feel the tension in the small of your back and your knees? With your chest thrust forward, they have to work hard to keep you balanced.

On the other hand, if a woman is shy, struggling with life and self-conscious about her breasts, she may round her shoulders forward to hide her chest. Her hip joints then become her physical center of balance. Round your shoulders forward to hide your chest and walk around the room. Feel the hip joints tighten to compensate for the rounded shoulders? As you walk you probably can't swing your legs freely from the hip joints. You sort of shuffle along.

By finding the physical center of a person's psychological objective in life you will not only discover how that person's ego, libido and id physically express themselves, you will also discover that the physical center of balance of a person is a counterbalance to that person's psychological center.

Initiating Inner Feelings

When you move around while establishing both your character's physical center and psychological center, you will suddenly begin to feel that you are that character. Move again using a combination of psychological center and physical center of balance. As you move, don't you begin to feel like a different person?

As I move with the trunk of my body thrust forward and the physical center of balance on my toes I feel aggressive, maybe compulsive or driven. When I move with my chest thrust forward and my center of balance in the small of my back and my knees, I feel both aggressive and defensive at the same time. It is as if I were balancing a devil-may-care attitude with a look-but-don't-touch attitude. As I move with my shoulders rounded forward and my physical center of balance in my hip joints, I feel shy but hopeful that someone will help me turn myself out toward society and stop me from turning myself in, away from society.

Don't Leave Yourself Out of the Creation of Your Character

Establishing a physical center of balance, psychological center combination that is different from your own will begin an inner monologue if you let it. Using the same combination of physical and psychological centers as I use will not make you feel exactly as I feel and that is because we are different people to begin with. Remember, you can't leave yourself out of the creation of your character. You aren't turning yourself into somebody else; you are making changes in yourself, adapting yourself, so that the character you are creating can become you. In that way your character remains a human being, not an idea of a human being or a physical caricature of a human being. When you use physical and psychological centers to help you create a character, let yourself think and feel as you think and feel.

Exercise: Psychological Gesture

Michael Chekhov, a nephew of playwright Anton Chekhov, was a fine acting teacher. The exercise that is most often associated with him is called Psychological Gesture. I present the use of Psychological Gesture to my students as part of their work on manifesting an image of their character by establishing that character's psychological center.

After you have established a multidimensional sense-memory image of your character, including his psychological center while lying down in concentration, get up and begin to move as your character in a limited space approximately six feet by six feet. Begin to create objects your character might have at hand. Involve them in an activity.

Before you begin this exercise, a class member of whose identity you are unaware should be picked to suddenly enter your space when he feels you have physically established your character and you are behaving in character.

Stay relaxed and concentrated on establishing and maintaining your character's balance of psychological center with a physical center. Involve yourself in your activity. Let obstacles to the activity happen. Need to do what you are doing. When your unknown partner suddenly enters your work space, allow yourself to react as your character wants to react. If you have been relaxed, concentrated and in character, you will immediately physically, and perhaps vocally, react to this intrusion.

As soon as your partner or your teacher is aware of your character's physical reaction to the intrusion, one of them should say "Freeze!"

Your in-character reaction to the intrusion may be large and dramatic or slight and not immediately obvious. In both cases, however, the reaction is an important physical expression of your character's psychological objective in life. It is your character's physical expression of his emotional response to an unexpected intrusion in his life. It is your character's Psychological Gesture. Your vocal response to that intrusion is an accompaniment to your physical response. Concentrate your attention on the physical response.

Your Psychological Gesture will be closely associated with your psychological center and your physical center of balance. The person who moves through life with the trunk of his body thrust forward might turn toward the intruder, grip the floor with his toes in a concerted effort to maintain balance, bend his knees, and thrust his trunk further forward in an I'm-going-to-tackle-you attitude.

That person might, however, straighten up and release his habitually aggressive posture. Then you have discovered that your character is outwardly aggressive but inwardly lacks confidence. His Psychological Gesture is saying, "Hello. What can I do for you?" rather than, "Look out or I'll knock you off your feet!" Either Psychological Gesture will be useful in building your character's role.

Psychological Gesture Used in a Production of Maxim Gorki's "The Lower Depths"

When I directed Gorki's *The Lower Depths,* I had each actor do a Psychological Gesture exercise. Almost all the exercises were successful. They established organic physical expressions of the character's psychological objectives in life.

Natasha is a shy but sexually and religiously passionate young woman. Her Psychological Gesture turned out to be a folding of the hands in prayer over her breasts. After the actress had established this Psychological Gesture by doing a Psychological Gesture exercise, the gesture became an organic part of her character's physical expression without the actress being conscious that this was happening. When Natasha was frightened or confused or emotionally aroused you would see her hands begin to fold in prayer. If the moment of challenge continued, the prayerful hands would rise to cover her chest.

Vaska Papel, the young thief, is an aggressive, violent-tempered street person. Our Vaska carried a knife strapped to his side by his belt. His Psychological Gesture was a crouch, weight on toes, feet separated with one foot forward and the other back, hands ready, one for the knife, the other for defense. All of this happened quickly and fluidly. Nothing moved more than a couple of inches but when Vaska was startled or angry or challenged in any way, you could feel the tension in the audience in reaction to Vaska's body language. Everyone was aware that Vaska might erupt with physical violence at any moment. When the challenge was over, Vaska relaxed into his normal lazy, graceful, catlike physical attitude.

On closing night I asked the actor playing Vaska if he was aware of how many times, in that night's performance, he had used Vaska's Psychological Gesture. He said that he was unaware that he had used it at all. After you have established a Psychological Gesture, don't plan to use it as specific times. Don't score it into the margins of your script. Once you have established a character's Psychological Gesture, your body will know what to do without your mind telling it what to do. Let a character's Psychological Gesture happen when it wants to during the normal process of building and performing a role.

"AS IFS" EXERCISES

I have already spoken to you about the use of "As Ifs" to help you create characters in farcical, symbolist, surrealistic and absurd plays. Because some of the characters in such plays are strange or exotic or dream-like or nightmarish or fantastic or unreal, you are going to have to use your imagination to create them. The use of "As Ifs" will help to bring your imagination alive. You may also have to use "As Ifs" in creating certain aspects of the behavior of real life characters in tragedies and comedies when that behavior seems unusual or eccentric.

Your Imagination As an "Af If" Sensory Process

You already know that an actor's imagination is a process built on the creative use of an actor's storehouse of sense-memories. The use of "As Ifs" is a research process. It is either a search through an actor's sensory experiences of the past or an exploration of new sensory experiences. Once the "As If" is established it becomes part of the process of manifesting or putting together or bringing alive your images of a character.

Exercise: "As If" Child

Some characters will immediately seem childlike to you. The playwright has them say and do childish things but when you say and do these things you feel foolish or inhibited. If this is the case, you can use an "As If" child exercise to give you permission or to free you to allow your character to behave with specific childlike behavior.

The child you know best is the child you once were. Bring yourself back to a specific time and place in your childhood. Let yourself play and behave in that place as you did when you were four or five years old. Let your childhood self play and behave in that place for an extended length of time and then turn the place into a kindergarten or a day care center and let your childhood self interact with the other children.

After you have recreated yourself as a child, immediately lie down on your back on the floor and relax, close your eyes and watch on your inner sense-memory screen the character on which you are working in the midst of an habitual or everyday activity. Chronologically and physically your character is the age he would be during the time frame of the play. Your character is dressed as he would dress. Your character is in a place where you have seen him before, but your character is moving and talking and behaving just as you did as a child.

Let your character have the energy and the thoughts and feelings you had as a child. As a child, you probably changed very quickly, without a sense of transition, from one activity to the next. You probably had very little patience in overcoming the obstacles to what you were doing. The time span of your concentration on one thing or another was very brief. Let your character behave exactly as if he were four or five years old.

What If You Didn't Have a Typical Childhood

Whether or not you have had a typical childhood you very well may need to reproduce behavior that is recognizable as childlike behavior. If you had an adult sort of a childhood, then study the behavior of a child who does behave as most children do.

Spend a couple of hours with the child. Play with him until you are instilled with the child's energy. Don't try to copy what the child does or to mimic the child. Match his change of activity and concentration. When you try to do something that demands hand-to-eye coordination try not to allow your thumbs to work easily in opposition to your fingers. Remove the adult strength and coordination from your legs. Allow yourself to feel the frustration of not being able to do some of the things you want to do. Don't dwell on your frustration. Quickly find something else to do. Above all else, try to have fun and to relate to the child with whom you are playing as a fellow child.

You will soon be worn to a frazzle but you will have experienced firsthand what you didn't experience as a child. As soon as possible, use the sense-memories of your experience as part of the image of the childlike character you will create. After you have reproduced childhood behavior and after you have laid down, relaxed and watched on your inner sense-memory screen your character behave like a four- or five-year-old, get up and do an improvisation with your scene partner. Do an improvisation that involves your characters in a relationship and an activity that could have taken place some time before the play takes place. Let your character behave as if he were four or five years old.

Adapting Your Childlike Behavior to an Adult World

Now, you have freed yourself as your childlike character to do the things you were too inhibited to do before you went through the "As If" exercise. Behaving as if you were a child within the framework of the life of an adult character, however, can be an exercise in ridiculousness. That may be just what you want in the creation of a subhuman or farcical character who is a celebrator of life. You can now make slight adjustments in your childlike behavior to fit your overall image of your character.

Most childlike characters in realistic comedies and tragedies, however, have the intentions and inner monologues of a young child but their behavior and the doings that fulfill those intentions and inner monologues have, over time, adapted themselves to the adult world. Unless you are an adult portraying a child, as in Caryl Churchill's play *Cloud Nine,* you will have to allow your character to grow up enough to fit into the dramatic situation of the play in which you are working.

Babe in Beth Henley's *Crimes of the Heart* is childlike but she is not a child. She has been married and has lived in a normal small town, middle-class society for twenty four years. You can have her think childish thoughts and do everything as if she were a child but to the degree which will make her believable as someone who has had twenty years to learn how to subdue her childish impulses. If you know the play, however, you know there are times when she is unable to subdue those impulses.

Exercise: "As If" Intoxicated

If you have never been under the influence of alcohol and you don't want to have that experience, don't use intoxicated "As Ifs".

By intoxicated I mean being under the influence of alcohol to the point where you behave more freely, spontaneously and openly than you would normally. If you have been intoxicated you have probably talked about things and done things you would not have talked about or done when you were sober. Recreating this sort of behavior can be very useful to an actor.

If, however, you get depressed, angry, obnoxious, or destructive when you are intoxicated, don't use these "As Ifs". That would be like using a traumatic experience as an affective memory. If you need to create harsh and aggressive behavior, use an actors' concentration or sense-memory that won't make you feel guilty or ashamed of yourself.

There are many modern plays in which the playwright or the director wants a character to be intoxicated. If you don't want to use a sense-memory of being intoxicated, you are going to have to use a sense-memory of another sort of high that is similar to being intoxicated. For some people, winning a game or a sporting event can be an experience that frees them to express themselves with spontaneity and without inhibitions.

Your character doesn't have to have been drinking within the story line of the play for you to put this "As If" to good use. You can use it to free yourself to create spontaneous, uninhibited, histrionic or silly behavior for a character who, within the story line of the play, is supposed to be sober.

Manifesting the "As If"

The technique of using "As Ifs" is always the same. You work with specific sense-memories toward specific character behavior and thought processes. To use an "As If" Intoxicated, lie down, close your eyes, relax, and relive a specific intoxicated experience. Remember on your inner sense-memory screen all the details of that experience. Then, watch your character behave on your sense-memory screen as if he were intoxicated.

Get up and do an improvisation with your scene partner and allow your character to behave as if he were intoxicated. As you are doing your improvisation physicalize drinking a couple of alcoholic drinks. Let your body and mind feel a specific stimulation.

Don't actually get intoxicated before an improvisation, a rehearsal or a performance. You won't be able to concentrate or do your actors' work. You won't be in control of your character's behavior and thoughts. If you are using the playwright's words, you won't be able to remember them.

After you have finished the improvisation, sit, relax and re-member the intoxicated behavior that would be useful to your character. Score intoxicated "As If" moments into your text. Once again, you must vary the degree to which you use the "As If". If you are creating a character who isn't supposed to be intoxicated, you are going to have to use the "As If" only to free your character's behavior and to allow him to become spontaneous, free and open. You are going to have to remove the aspects of your behavior that would make your character actually seem intoxicated.

Exercise: "As If" Animal

Using "As If" animal has been very useful for me as a director and an actor. When I have done all the basic work I can think to do on a character and there still seems to be an important element of that character's personality missing, I try recreating that character as if he were a specific animal.

In the production of Euripides' *Iphigenia in Tauris* that I directed, the actors playing King Taos' soldiers were not physically big enough or threatening enough. I had them sit, relax, close their eyes and remember the classic 1933 King Kong movie and the size and specific physical behavior of King Kong. I had them turn them-selves into gorillas just as they had done many times in their physical warming up exercises. They bent forward from their hip joints and knees. Their arms hung heavily from their sides. Their chins hung heavily from their jaw hinges.

For three rehearsals they played the soldiers as if they were gorillas. Their physical behavior became aggressive, powerful and frightening. The actors playing the soldiers told me that they were beginning to think like animals. When they gave orders, they roared them. The actresses playing the priestesses told me that when the soldiers were present they were intimidated. They were hesitant to do what they had planned to do. Obviously, I now had the relationship of barbarian captors and priestess captives that the play needed. The soldiers had created the physical strength and sense of physical threat that they needed to create.

Humanizing the "As If"
In the next rehearsals, I had the soldiers gradually turn them-selves into humans. They maintained their sense of strength and aggression. When they spoke, their words still had a good chest resonant roar. They had turned, however, from gorillas to animal-like barbarians and all they had done was to straighten up slightly from their knees and hip joints.

Study Specific Sense-Memories

If you use an animal "As If ", take the time to study the specific behavior of a specific animal. Go to a zoo where the animals are in contained fields rather than in cages. Watch the behavior of domestic pets. I remember Lee Strasberg saying that we could become good actors by watching closely for a full day everything that a cat did. I think he meant that he had never witnessed a better combination of relaxation and concentration than he saw in the behavior of a cat.

When in doubt about how to bring a character alive, use an animal "As If ". Be sure, however, to study specific elements of the behavior of an animal whose personality reminds you of your character's personality. Don't use general concepts of an animal you haven't studied. You will only cartoon animal behavior.

In other words, if you want your character to behave as if he were a cat, don't play gracefulness and quickness. Study the behavior of a specific cat and put your sense-memories of that cat's behavior to use in creating your character's behavior. Unless you are playing a cat character in the musical *Cats,* don't forget to turn your character back into a catlike human being after you have had that character behave as if he were a cat.

Exercise: "As If " Psychotic

From the time I decided to make my living as an actor, I have thought about playing Shakespeare's Hamlet. I have never played Hamlet in a production of *Hamlet* but I have worked on the part and I have played Hamlet in acting classes and at auditions and I have coached other actors in the part. The part never completely came alive for me until I thoroughly considered what Hamlet, just after he has been confronted with the ghost of his murdered father, says to his best friend, Horatio. He says:

> *How strange or odd soe'er I bear myself,—*
> *As I perchance hereafter shall think meet*
> *To put an antic disposition on,—*
> *That you, at such times seeing me, never shall,*
> *With arms encumber'd thus, or this head-shake,*
> *Or by pronouncing of some doubtful phrase,*
> *As, 'Well, well, we know,' or, 'We could, an if we would;'*
> *Or, 'If we list to speak,' or, 'There be, an if they might;'*
> *Or such ambiguous giving out, to note*
> *That you know aught of me.*

(*The Tragedy of Hamlet, Prince of Denmark,* Yale University Press, 1954, New Haven, Act I, pages 169-179.)

I interpret this passage to mean that Hamlet intends to pretend he is crazy in order to disguise his intention to take revenge on his father's murderer, his uncle Claudius.

I believe that Shakespeare had studied the behavior of specific insane people and that he has Hamlet use the sense-memories of this behavior to pretend to be mad. I also believe that very quickly Shakespeare has Hamlet become possessed of the madness that he was at first only pretending and that Shakespeare used his study of specific insane people to create Hamlet's actual madness. Whether Hamlet only pretends madness or actually does go insane, the actor building and playing the part must learn to behave as if he were psychotic.

If I were to direct *Hamlet*, I would ask the actor building the role of Hamlet to use specific psychotic "As Ifs" to create the character. I would ask the actor to find specific psychotic behavior to fit Hamlet's behavior in the American Psychiatric Association's *Diagnostic and Statistical Manual of Mental Disorders, the Third Edition - Revised*, commonly referred to as the *DSM-III-R* (Washington, DC 1987).

In the case of psychotic behavior, you, of course, must not use sense-memories, if you are unlucky enough to have them, of your own psychotic behavior. You must never use traumatic sense-memories. If you have had a psychotic experience, don't use psychotic "As Ifs". The *DSM-III-R*, however, describes in detail the specific behavior of people with specific mood disorders. An actor who has not suffered mood disorders can, without actually experiencing the mental disorder that results in psychotic behavior in real life, use the *DSM-III-R's* descriptions to create psychotic behavior for a character.

Having myself matched Hamlet's behavior and thought patterns to specific sympoms of mental disorders in the *DSM-III-R*, I know the actor would find that much of his character's behavior would be diagnosed today, not as pretended madness, but as actual schizophrenic behavior.

Hamlet often converses in nonsequitur phrases. He becomes slovenly. He has delusions of persecution. He is socially withdrawn, depressed and preoccupied with death. He bursts with anger for no apparent reason. Finally, he hallucinates; he sees an apparition that other characters cannot see. All of this behavior the *DSM-III-R* confirms as schizophrenic behavior.

The *DSM-III-R* also describes specific schizophrenic behavior that Shakespeare does not dramatize as Hamlet's behavior. For instance, the *DSM-III-R* says that schizophrenic behavior can be accompanied by "the voice that is usually monotonous and face immobile." It also speaks of "apparently purposeless and stereotyped, excited motor movements not influenced by external stimuli." This specific psychotic behavior can be added by the actor to the building of the role of Hamlet.

I do not advocate playing Hamlet as if he were a raving maniac. If Hamlet thought he was going mad, he would do everything he could to try to prove to himself that he was still sane. Whether or not Hamlet is insane, he is definitely the model of a Renaissance man. He is quick-witted, full of humor, sensitive, athletic and proud. He is a man of infinite proportions.

All of the obstacles to Hamlet's struggle with life are sizeable and important. If he puts too much energy into his struggle, if he constantly allows his madness to get the better of him, or if he overplays his pretense of madness, his behavior will become ludicrous, even ridiculous. Hamlet is and should be one of the most sympathetic characters in all of theatre's history. He is the man with whom all men and all women of all times can identify. He is the best and worst of all men and women.

Therefore, the playing of Hamlet should be done with extreme subtlety and understanding. His outbursts of maniacal energy should be saved for important moments such as his killing of an innocent old man, Polonius, or his burst of emotion as he vicariously kills Claudius in the "O what a rogue and peasant slave am I!" solioquy, or his leap into Ophelia's grave and his fight with Ophelia's brother, Laertes, in the grave. Hamlet's innate gentleness, intelligence and humor should constantly come to the surface to oppose his actual or pretended madness.

You don't have to be a character actor to be a successful supporting actor. Many straight actors make good careers out of playing supportive roles. (Author Carlton Colyer, left, playing a scene with Charles Coburn in <u>You Can't Take It With You</u> by Moss Hart and George S. Kaufman, Ivoryton, Connecticut.)

4. Getting a Part

TYPECASTING

Typecasting is a fact of life in American theatre and movies and television. Typecasting, however, doesn't have to mean that when you have played a successful role you are condemned to play that sort of role for the rest of your career. That is deadly typecasting. Being a victim of deadly typecasting means playing either a struggler or a celebrator, in the same dramatic form, in the same period of style, over and over again.

STRAIGHT ACTORS AND CHARACTERS ACTORS

The typecasting that can work for you is establishing yourself as either a straight actor or a character actor. There is a ninety-five per cent chance that you are one or the other. Very few actors are both. When you have discovered which type you are by experimenting in scene classes, then, you can work to become all you can be at that type of acting. You can make yourself into a good, useful actor. Only when you have the reputation as a good, useful actor can you be sure of getting one part after another. Find out, by working on many different roles, in all the dramatic forms, in many different periods of style, whether you are happier working as a character actor or a straight actor.

The actor who I define as a character actor is the sort of actor who has a facility for using himself to create many different characters, none of whom resemble the actor as much as they do somebody else. The actor who I define as a straight actor is the actor who creates characters who resemble the actor more than they do anybody else. A straight actor's personality is too powerful to lose itself in the process of creating a character.

Good straight actors, however, bring their own multidimensional personalities to their actors' work, and when they create

Find out, by working on many different roles, in all the dramatic forms, whether you are happier working as a character actor or a straight actor. (Left to right: Franklin Cover, Betty White, and author Carlton Colyer in <u>Light Up the Sky</u> *by Moss Hart, The Royal Poinciance Theatre, Palm Beach, Florida.)*

characters, they are willing to allow elements of their personalities that rarely express themselves in their everyday lives to express themselves in their actors' work.

As long as you are creating believable, multidimensional human characters that fit the roles for which they are created, it doesn't matter whether you undergo a complete personality change every time you create a new character. If you play yourself well and you have a facility for finding roles that resemble you, you can consider yourself an accomplished actor and you will be accepted by directors as an accomplished straight actor.

SUPPORTING ACTORS

For every star there are dozens of actors who play leads who never become stars. You don't have to become a star or to play leads to become a success. There are always ten good supporting roles for every leading role. Unless they are stars, leading actors don't get cast as often as do supporting actors. In my mind, the actor who wins the Best Supporting Actor Oscar or Tony or Emmy is just as successful an actor as is the actor who wins the Best Leading Actor awards.

More important than anything else, you don't have to be a character actor to be a successful supporting actor. Many straight actors make good careers out of playing supportive roles. Some straight actors and character actors, especially in theatre, go back and forth between playing supporting roles and leading roles.

EXAMPLES OF TYPES OF ACTORS

Here are some names of actors whose work you should study and be challenged by. You should not try to copy or to mimic the work of any of these actors, but by watching their work, you can see if you agree about the general type of actor they are.

Some of these actors you can see today working on the stage, in movies or on television. Some of them are dead. All of them, however, have made movies. If you can't see them today on stage or on a television show or in a recently released movie, you can get a VCR tape of a movie they have made or you can look for them in movies shown on television.

In my opinion, they are all good actors. They never fail to create interesting, multidimensional believably human characters. They avoid doing demonstrational, mechanical or manipulative work even when they are on prime time, comedy television shows on which many times there is forced farcical acting.

197

Some leading actors on the list are also well-known for playing supporting roles and some of the supporting actors occasionlly played leads. Often, actors who have been straight leading actors or character leading actors when they were young become supporting actors when they get older.

Straight Leading Actors:

Alan Alda, Anne Baxter, Lucille Ball, Ingrid Bergman, Humphrey Bogart, Richard Burton, Charles Chaplin, Montgomery Clift, Gary Cooper, Tom Cruise, Ossie Davis, Henry Fonda, John Garfield, James Garner, Greer Garson, Katharine Hepburn, William Holden, Jack Lemmon, Shirley MacLaine, Marcello Mastroianni, Robert Mitchum, Marilyn Monroe, Paul Newman, Sidney Poitier, Sir Michael Redgrave, Barbara Stanwyck and Susannah York.

Straight Supporting Actors:

Martin Balsam, Anne Bancroft, Leo Barnes, Ed Begley, Charles Bronson, Gary Burghoff, Charles Coburn, Gladys Cooper, Robert DeNiro, Leif Erickson, Barry Fitzgerald, Louis Gosset, Hugh Griffith, Jack Hawkins, Trevor Howard, John Houseman, Kim Hunter, Shirley Jones, Dorothy Malone, Robert Morley, Patricia Neal, Robert Newton, Edmond O'Brien, Jack Palance, Rhea Perlman, Anthony Quinn, Lee Remick, Dame Margaret Rutherford, John Thaw, Billy Dee Williams and Betty White.

Character Leading Actors:

Edward Asner, Richard Attenborough, Richard Burton, Jeremy Brett, Lee J. Cobb, James Dean, Sandy Dennis, Dame Edith Evans, Albert Finney, Sir John Gielgud, Sir Alec Guinness, Greta Garbo, Greer Garson, Whoopi Goldberg, Robert Hardy, Helen Hayes, Dame Wendy Hiller, Dustin Hoffman, Vivian Leigh, Leo McKern, Shirley MacLaine, Anna Magnani, John Malkovich, James Mason, Paul Muni, Peter O'Toole, Geraldine Page, Maggie Smith, Kim Stanley, Maureen Stapleton, Meryl Streep, Margaret Sullavan and Max Von Sydow.

Character Supporting Actors:

Jack Albertson, Harry Andrews, Alan Arkin, Dame Peggy Ashcroft, Ethel Barrymore, Anne Baxter, Ward Bond, Walter Brennan, Roscoe Lee Brown, Donald Crisp, Mildred Dunnock, Lee Grant, George Grizzard, Van Heflin, Joan Hickson, Josephine Hull, Walter Houston, Cloris Leachman, Roddy McDowall, Nancy Marchand, Lee Marvin, Walter Matthau, John Mills, Thomas Mitchell, Arthur O'Connell, Estelle Parsons, Edward Petheridge, Vanessa Redgrave, Sir Ralph Richardson, Anne Revere, Jason Robards, Flora Robson, David Ogden Stiers, Donald Sutherland, Shelly Winters and Teresa Wright.

Don't associate socially with the other actors auditioning. If you do you will run the risk of assuming their nervous tension. (Young Actors, Colorado Springs, Colorado.)

AUDITIONING

As I have said, auditioning or reading for a part seldom involves doing an audition monologue unless you volunteer to do one. Auditioning also seldom involves any time for preparation. Only established name actors are given scripts ahead of time. Most of the time, you will arrive for an audition, a script will be handed to you and you will be assigned a character and part of a scene from that script that will serve as the material with which you will audition. Usually the passage assigned to you will involve a dialogue between two characters. Usually a stage manager will read the part of the character playing opposite your character. If you arrive for your audition at the exact time scheduled for your audition, you may be asked to read five or ten minutes after you have arrived.

Count on the fact that you will audition very close to the time you are scheduled. Get to the audition early and score some actors' work to the dialogue assigned to you. Don't expect an auditioner to talk to you before you begin your reading. Ask the person who hands you the script who your character is, where the scene takes place, when it takes place and what your character is doing. Even if you only get partial answers to your questions, you will be better off than if you had no 4 W's information.

Don't associate socially with the other actors auditioning. If you do, you will run the risk of assuming their nervous tension.

Don't waste your time trying to memorize any of the words. Read the whole passage a couple of times. Familiarize yourself with the cues to your dialogue. Then you can listen for your cues without constantly staring at the script. Pencil in some simple scoring. Use your imagination and create whatever of the 4 W's that hasn't been given to you.

Don't be afraid to score in specific physical states of being your character can manifest. Decide what is up and out front of the acting area to which you can relate the playwright's words. Above all else, be specific about your character's relationship with the other character or characters in the scene. Decide on a very specific intention that involves what your character wants or needs from the other character or characters in the scene.

At least five minutes before your scheduled reading, warm up your limbs and joints and your voice. Then, do a thorough relaxation exercise.

You will probably read in an office or in an empty studio or on an empty stage. There may just be a pilot light and a darkened theatre to greet you if you audition on an empty stage. Introduce yourself to your auditioners if you can locate them, and be prepared to immediately begin your reading. Assume that the stage manager's reading of the other part or parts has the meaning and feeling behind it that it should have. Let yourself react to the other character or characters. Try to get the other character or characters to do what your character wants them to do.

If there are no obstacles to your getting what your character wants, create them. Don't however, attempt to physicalize objects and to involve your character in an activity. You can pretend that your script is an object that is important to the action of the scene. If there is a chair available, your character might sit down in it or stand up on it for a moment. If it fits the dramatic situation you might have your character sit down or lie down or kneel on the floor. In other words, don't be afraid to allow your character to express himself physically as well as verbally.

If the stage manager is reading the parts of a couple of characters, put one of the characters about six feet to one side of the stage manager. Don't be afraid to upstage the stage manager and to make yourself available to the auditioners. Let your character move away from or toward the other characters but make your moves relate directly to your character's intentions. Stand still and connect the playwright's words to a sense-memory image up and out front of the acting area. If you become tense, pause and do a very quick relaxation exercise.

Don't try to pick up cues or to give the reading pace or tempo. Try to look at passages in the script, not just words. Look ahead to your cues and then let your character listen and react to what the other character or characters are saying. Don't be afraid to pause and to take a look at the script.

When you have finished reading the assigned passage, never apologize for your work. If the auditioner says nothing to you, ask if you can do a two-and-a-half-minute monologue that relates to the work you have just done and that you feel will reinforce that work.

If the auditioner likes your reading of the assigned passage, he may talk to you and give you some direction and ask you to read the passage again or to read another passage involving the same character or an entirely different character. If this happens, listen carefully to the direction given, interpret it as actors' work and ask for any missing 4 W's. Don't ask too many questions, just enough to get your character connected to specific actors' work. If you are to read a new passage, you probably will be given a brief time to read over the passage and to prepare it. Put the time to use. If you are to redo the original passage, don't let the stage manager rush you, but pause no more than thirty seconds. Relate the direction given to your own choices of actors' work, say, "Okay, let's go" to the stage manager and go for it.

If an auditioner spends a good deal of time having you reread passages or having you read new passages from the script, and you haven't done a monologue of your own, don't offer to do a monologue. You have had all the opportunity you can expect to get. When I knew an audition was over, I said, "Thank you very much" and meant it, and I left. I figured I would let my work stand on its own.

REHEARSALS

In normal circumstances you will be given a script at least a week before rehearsal begins. Usually, you will have time before a first rehearsal of a play to do your research. Once you are in rehearsal, however, you won't have enough time or energy to do much research.

At a first rehearsal most directors will explain their concept of the play to the cast. Then, they will have the cast sit around a large table and read the play through once or twice. Next, most directors will begin to block the play. Very few directors will get into lengthy discussions about meanings and motivations. Discussions like these with one actor will waste the time of the other actors. There is no reason for you to be dependent on a director for anything but his objective appraisal of the work you will do. You are thoroughly prepared to find your own meanings and motivations. Only you need know the fifth W, why your character does what he does.

Taking Direction

A director's blocking of a play as a first step in rehearsal can be a deadly and inhibiting experience if you let it be. Do your homework. Work on scenes to be blocked at least a couple of days beforehand. Work on scenes as you would in scene class when you didn't have a director. Be prepared. Score in your 4 W's. Try your best to put the director's blocking to work, but, if the director's blocking seems impossible after a couple of attempts to use it, don't be afraid to ask the director to let you show him a specific piece of blocking you have worked out. If your blocking or choice of doing an activity works better than what the director has given you, it is an insecure director who won't accept the improvement. Don't forget, however, that, from a director's point of view, your work must not only bring your character alive, it must also help to bring a scene and ultimately the whole play alive.

Don't ever contradict or argue with a director. Keep trying to cooperate and to do your own creative work at the same time. If, after you do a scene or a section of a scene, the director gives you some direction and asks you to go off and work on the scene yourself, it is not cheating or bad manners to go and work with the other actor or actors in the scene and to combine your creative work with the director's directions. When a good director sees a piece of work that isn't exactly what he directed but is in the spirit of what he directed and is better than what he had in mind, the director will welcome that work.

Fulfilling and Committing

Don't forget to warm up and to relax before every rehearsal. Work slowly and patiently. Put the director's direction to the best use possible. Strive to become part of the ensemble, one of a company of actors, all of whom are doing their best to bring the entire dramatic event excitingly and multidimensionally alive. Do your homework. Work overtime with the actors in your scenes. Keep scoring and rescoring your text. Try to adapt your work to the work of the other actors, but give them a chance to adapt their work to your work. Even when you are in your first production, if you have been thoroughly trained and if you are doing your work thoroughly, there is no reason to take direction from another actor. By the same token, you have no right to try to direct another actor.

About a week before dress rehearsal, set your scoring, and, in each subsequent rehearsal, try to fulfill that scoring and to work moment to moment without stopping to rework anything. If you have changes to make, make them after rehearsal as you do your homework. Day by day, commit yourself to what you have chosen to do. Fulfill each beat. Make your transitions. Don't anticipate. By dress rehearsal your work should be at the stage where, when you as your character are involved in the dramatic situation, you are no longer conscious of doing actors' work. You are living the part you have created. You are playing your role.

You now need an audience to let you know if you are playing that role as believably and interestingly as possible.

WORKING IN FRONT OF AN AUDIENCE

There is an implication of audience manipulation within the phrase, "to give a performance." If you welcome an audience as a participant in the dramatic event and you play your role as you conceived it in rehearsal, audience reaction will support and encourage what your character is doing. The audience will react as human beings to a believable human situation. As you are working in front of an audience, you must not anticipate what their reaction will be or should be. If you begin to indicate to an audience or to tell an audience what your character is doing, you are actually stepping out of character. You are communicating as the actor, not the character. If you do this, you will be interrupting and disturbing the audience's through line of involvement in the dramatic situation.

A good actor goes over the work he has done in front of an audience a few hours after he has finished that work. In retrospect, if the actor feels that a moment or a series of moments in the performance could have been clearer, more available, funnier or more poignant to an audience, the actor should rethink that moment or series of moments. He should also rethink moments in which the character's intentions and actions didn't get the results from the other characters that they might have. The actor should then rescore his work for the next performance. If the changes you make in scoring affects the work of other actors, let those actors know about the changes you intend to make. Once rehearsals are over, an actor may not change a piece of blocking without the permission of the stage manager. Good actors never stop working on their parts. In front of an audience, they work moment to moment but they don't try to rescore on the spur of the moment.

There is no question that opening nights are special. You can anticipate that an opening night will add energy to your work. You must focus that wonderful energy and not let it run away with you. On opening nights, take longer to warm up and to relax than you would normally take. About ten minutes before your cue to go on, prepare. Let your character live through the event that occurs just before the dramatic action takes place. Create specific physical states of being that your character will bring to the dramatic action. When the curtain goes up or you get your cue to go on, connect yourself to the first beat of your first scene and give yourself to the work you did in your last rehearsals.

If you experience actors' tension or you feel opening night energy running away with you, pause and in character, do a quick relaxation exercise. Above all let yourself have fun playing the role as you conceived it.

READING REVIEWS

Read your reviews. Some actors will tell you that they never read reviews and that you are a fool if you do. They are not telling you the truth and you are not a fool to read your reviews. When a reviewer singles you out in his review that reviewer will have revealed an interest in your work. If the reviewer has said something negative about that work, he has probably said it with the hope that it will help you realize the potential for good work that the reviewer sees in you.

You must always, however, be objective about criticism. There are few critics that know as much about actors' work as you know. What a critic says is good about your work may be what is bad about it and vice versa. The only damning thing a critic or a reviewer can do to you is leave you out of a review. It is a critic's responsibility to say something about every aspect of a production that is worthy of criticism. Even when you play a small part, if you do the work you now know how to do, you will deserve each and every critic's notice.

If you get left out of a review, I would drop the reviewer a note and ask why this happened. I did this once and found out that what the critic had said about my work, because of the length of his review, had been edited out of the review when it was published. The critic sent me the passage that had been edited out and it glowed with praise for me and several other actors.

WORKING IN FRONT OF A CAMERA

Working in front of a camera and working on stage are very similar. The first thing you realize is that you do the same actors' work in both mediums. You have to modify that work, however, in front of a camera.

First, you must reduce the size and strength of your physical and vocal expression. This becomes immediately obvious to you as soon as you realize that the camera lens and the microphone in close-up and medium shots is no more than ten feet away and as close to you as a few inches. Long shots with the camera as much as fifty feet away you can treat as if you were on stage. You will, however, never be asked to project your voice that distance. If they want to pick up and single out your voice in a long shot, they will either pin a lavaliere microphone on you or they will boom out a microphone directly over your head.

The concentration on a sensory image you would customarily place a number of feet up and out toward a theatre audience, you must place an inch or two to either side of the camera lens in a close-up shot. If the sensory concentration is specific, the lens will see the truth and dimension of your facial expression as no theatre audience ever could.

Relaxation, especially in a close-up shot, is essential. When the director says, "Roll camera, roll sound," you should do a quick relaxation exercise. Be sure to release any tension in your eyes, forehead and eyebrows. As you move your head using the neck's seven vertebrae and you take a deep, gentle breath with your bellows, close your eyes and imagine dark blue velvet in front of them. When the director says, "Action," pause an instant, open your eyes, connect to a pleasant or unpleasant sensory image or an inner monologue and then speak or do what your character is required to do.

When you are shooting a major movie, the character to whom your character is speaking or reacting in a close-up probably won't actually be there. You are going to have to personalize him or her at a specific distance usually just behind the camera.

In a close-up and a medium shot, you are going to be asked to pay close attention to your position, even the angle of your head and the focus of your eyes. Only when you are relating eyeball to eyeball with another character would you look directly into the camera lens. In a medium shot, if you move into a position you must precisely hit your marks that are taped on the floor or the ground. When you move to one side or the other of your original marks or you sit down or stand up, you must do it slowly enough for the camera to pan with you and to follow focus.

Movies and television are much more a visual medium of expression than they are a verbal means of expression. Don't be afraid in a medium shot or a long shot to physically express your character's intentions. Let psychological gesture manifest itself. Use rehearsal time to bring the objects at hand to life. Create activity to fulfill intentions. Be physically and mentally relaxed when the camera is on, and that perfect geste, like Brando's use of Eva Marie Saint's gloves and the child's playground swing in *On the Waterfront,* will happen as if you hadn't consciously planned it to happen.

Getting used to the amount of rehearsal time will probably be your biggest problem doing work in front of a camera. In movies, the time spent rehearsing is usually the time between shots that is taken up with relighting, moving the camera and refocusing. Use the time. Establish your 4 W's. Find out especially where your character is and what objects are there to establish activity to fulfill intention. If you are shooting out of sequence in the dramatic action, find out what happens to your character just before and after the scene being shot.

If you aren't absolutely sure of your actor's technique, if you can't very quickly put that technique to use, the best you can do in front of a camera is to do mechanically what the director tells you to do. Not many directors will hire you again if they have to show you what to do.

BUILDING A CAREER

The first advice I have for you about becoming a working actor is to treat the whole process both as a business and a creative art. You become a professional, creative artist as soon as you have done

one good piece of work to prove that you are. When you have done two or three pieces of professional acting work and each piece of work has produced a multidimensional, interesting character that brought the playwright's words and the dramatic event alive, you will have a reputation for being dependable.

If, as you work, you relate to directors, writers, designers, producers, agents and technicians as fellow professional artists and you cherish being part of an ensemble of actors, you should have enough work to make your living in the theatre.

You may never become a star or a millionaire doing the work I have taught you, but you will discover hundreds of opportunities, in and out of professional theatre, to work as an actor. You will bring thought and sensitivity, love and happiness, the exicitement of being a creative artist not only into your own life but into the lives of thousands of people.

BIBLIOGRAPHY

Adair, Gilbert and Roddick, Nick, *A Night at the Pictures, Ten Decades of British Film.* London, Columbus, 1985.

Adler, Stella, *The Technique of Acting.* New York, Bantam, 1989.

Artaud, Antonin, *The Theatre and Its Double.* New York, Grove, 1958.

Atkinson, Brooks, *Broadway.* London, Cassell, 1970.

Bablet, Denis, *The Theatre of Edward Gordon Craig.* London, Eyre Methuen, 1981.

Bentley, Eric, *The Theory of the Modern Stage.* New York, Penguin, 1978.

Bentley, Eric, *What Is Theatre?* New York, Atheneum, 1968.

Blum, Daniel, *A Pictorial History of the American Theatre.* New York, Crown, 1972.

Blum, Daniel, *A New Pictorial History of the Talkies.* Putnam, G. P., 1968.

Brecht, Bertold, *Brecht on Theatre.* New York, Hill and Wang, 1977.

Brockett, Oscar, *History of the Theatre.* Boston, Allyn and Bacon, 1974.

Brook, Peter, *The Empty Space.* Harmondsworth, Penguin, 1977.

Brooks, Tim and Marsh, Earle, *The Complete Directory to Prime Time Network TV Shows 1946-Present.* New York, Ballantine, 1988.

Brustein, Robert, *The Theatre of Revolt.* Boston, Little Brown, 1964.

Brustein, Robert, *The Third Theatre.* New York, Simon and Schuster, 1970.

Burnett, T. A. J., *The Rise and Fall of a Regency Dandy.* Boston, Little Brown, 1981.

Chekhov, Michael, *To the Actor.* New York, Harper and Row, 1953.

Chinoy, Helen K., *Reunion, a Self Portrait of the Group Theatre.* Washington, The American Theatre Association, 1976.

Clurman, Harold, *The Fervent Years.* New York, Knopf, Alfred A., 1950.

Cohen, George M., *A History of American Art.* New York, Dell, 1971.

Cohen, Robert, *Acting Professionally.* Palo Alto, Mayfield, 1981.

Cole, Toby and Chinoy, Helen K., *Directors on Directing.* Indianapolis, Bobbs-Merrill, 1983.

Cook, Judith, *The National Theatre.* London, Harrap, 1976.

Cowie, Peter, Editor, *A Concise History of the Cinema,* 2 Vols. New York, Barnes H. S. 1971.

Crawford, Bartholow and Kern, Alexander and Needleman, Morriss, *American Literature.* New York, Barnes and Noble, 1969.

Dantchenko, Vladimir N., *My Life in the Russian Theatre.* New York, Theatre Arts Books, 1968.

Delgado, Alan, *Victorian Entertainment.* Newton Abbott, Victorian

Book Club, 1972.

Ducharte, Pierre L., *The Italian Comedy.* New York, Dover, 1966.

Dukore, Bernard F., *Dramatic Theory and Criticism.* New York, Holt, Rinehart and Winston, 1974.

Durant, Will, *The Story of Civilization,* 10 Vols. New York, Simon and Schuster, 1963.

Edwards, Christopher, *The London Theatre Guide 1576-1642.* London, Burlington, 1979.

Einstein, Alfred, *A Short History of Music.* New York, Vintage, 1954.

Erlanger, Phillipe, *The Age of Courts and Kings.* New York, Harper and Row, 1967.

Esslin, Martin, *An Anatomy of Drama.* London, Abacus, 1978.

Esslin, Martin, *The Theatre of the Absurd.* New York, Penguin, 1977.

Feldenkrais, Moshe, *Awareness Through Movement.* New York, Harper and Row, 1977.

Fraser, Antonia, *The Weaker Vessel.* New York, Knopf, Alfred A., 1984.

Garland, Madge and Black, Anderson and Kennett, Frances, *A History of Fashion.* New York, Quill, 1986.

Gassner, John and Allen, Ralph G., *Theatre and Drama in the Making,* 2 Vols. Boston, Houghton and Mifflin, 1964.

Glasstone, Victor, *Victorian and Edwardian Theatres.* London, Thames and Hudson, 1975.

Goldman, William, *The Season.* New York, Bantam, 1970.

Gorelik, Mordecai, *New Theatres for Old.* New York, Samuel French, 1947.

Grotowski, Jerzy, *Towards a Poor Theatre.* New York, Simon and Schuster, 1968.

Grun, Bernard, *The Timetables of History.* New York, Simon and Schuster, 1982.

Hagen, Uta, *Respect for Acting.* New York, Macmillan, 1978.

Harris, William H. and Levy, Judith S., Editors, *The New Columbia Encyclopedia,* New York, Lippincott, J. B., 1975.

Hartnoll, Phyllis, Editor, *The Oxford Companion to the Theatre.* Oxford, Oxford University Press, 1967.

Hayman, Ronald, *British Theatre Since 1955.* Oxford, Oxford University Press, 1979.

Henderson, Mary C., *Theatre in America.* New York, Abrams, H. N., 1988.

Hethman, Robert H., *Strasberg at the Actors Studio.* New York, Viking, 1968.

Hornby, Richard, *Script into Performance.* New York, Paragon, 1987.

Honri, Peter, *Working the Halls.* London, Futura, 1974.

Johnson, Otto, Editor, *The 1988 Information Please Almanac.* Boston, Houghton Mifflin, 1988.

Jones, Robert E., *The Dramatic Imagination.* New York, Theatre Arts

Books, 1969.

Katz, Ephraim, *The Film Encyclopedia.* New York, Growell, T. Y., 1979.

Knight, Arthur, *The Liveliest Art.* Bergenfield, The New American Library, 1957.

Korn, Jerry, Editor, *Seven Centuries of Art,* 28 Vols. New York, Time Life Books, 1970.

Ladurie, LeRoy, *Carnival in Romans.* New York, Braziller, George, 1980.

Lindsay, Dr. J., *A Short History of Science.* Garden City, Doubleday, 1959.

Linklater, Kristin, *Freeing the Natural Voice.* New York, Drama Book Publishers, 1976.

Lister, Margot, *Costume.* London, Barrie and Jenkins, 1977.

Loftis, John and Southern, Richard and Jones, Marion and Scouten, A. H., *The Revels History of Drama in English,* 8 Vols. London, Methuen, 1976.

McGaw, Charles, *Acting Is Believing.* New York, Holt, Rinehart and Winston, 1966.

Marshall, Herbert, *The Pictorial History of the Russian Theatre.* New York, Crown, 1977.

Meyerhold, Usevold, *Meyerhold on Theatre.* New York, Hill and Wang, 1981.

Moore, Sonia, *Training an Actor.* New York, Viking, 1968.

Muir, Frank, *An Irreverant and Almost Complete Social History of the Bathroom.* Briarcliff Manor, Stein and Day, 1983.

Nagler, M. A., *A Source Book in Theatrical History.* New York, Dover, 1959.

Nicoll, Allardyce, *British Drama.* New York, Harper and Row, 1978.

Oliver, Paul and Harrison, Max and Bolcom, William, *Gospel, Blues and Jazz.* New York, Norton, W. W., 1986.

Peacock, John, *Costume 1066-1966.* London, Thames and Hudson, 1986.

Russell, Douglas A., *Period Style in the Theatre.* Boston, Allyn and Bacon, 1980.

Sainer, Arthur, *The Radical Theatre Notebook.* New York, Avon, 1975.

Simonson, Lee, *The Stage Is Set.* New York, Theatre Arts Books, 1970.

Smith, Cecil and Litton, Glenn, *Musical Comedy in America.* New York, Theatre Arts Books, 1981.

Spolin, Viola, *Improvisation for the Theatre.* Evanston, Northwestern University Press, 1976.

Stanislavski, Constantin, *An Actor Prepares.* New York, Theatre Arts Books, 1970.

Stanislavksi, Constantin, *Building a Character.* New York, Theatre Arts Books, 1981.

Stanislavski, Constantin, *Creating a Role.* New York, Theatre Arts

Books, 1980.

Stanislavski, Constantin, *My Life in Art.* New York, Meridian, 1956.

Sweet, Jeffrey, *Something Wonderful Right Away.* New York, Avon, 1978.

Toporkov, Vasily O., *Stanislavsky in Rehearsal.* New York, Theatre Arts Books, 1979.

Tynan, Kenneth, *Curtains.* New York, Atheneum, 1961.

Vincent, Anne J., *History of Art.* New York, Barnes and Noble, 1969.

Westfeldt, Lulie, *F. Matthias Alexander, The Man and His Work.* Long Beach, Centerline, 1986.

Wildblood, John, *The Polite World.* London, Davis-Poynter, 1973.

Witt, Hubert, *Brecht As They Knew Him.* New York, International Publishers, 1977.

ABOUT THE AUTHOR
CARLTON COLYER

Though a graduate of Princeton and former head of drama at Syracuse in London, a professor of theatre at Brown University and the University of Rhode Island, Colyer is no academic. He is living testimony of the total actor and "Renaissance Man" of the real world.

He has been a roustabout with Ringling Brothers Circus, a captain in the United States Marine Corps, a salmon fisherman, a performer on Broadway and off-Broadway stages, on national television and in motion pictures.

His credits include over two hundred plays in which he has played both leads and supporting roles with many of theatre's greatest names: Tallulah Bankhead, Charles Coburn, Jane Fonda, June Havoc, Helen Hayes, Van Johnson, Jack Lemmon, Darren McGavin, Jane Morgan, Vincent Price, Gloria Swanson, Betty White and many more.

More than twenty years ago he transferred his energies from acting and directing to the teaching of acting. His students are adults, gifted teenagers, the underprivileged, the mentally retarded and the emotionally disturbed.

He has written many articles and guides on acting and professional theatre but there has never been time enough to do a complete book until this one.

Additional thanks to these actors and students for use of their photographs in this book:
Page 10, left to right: Melissa Shepherd, Karen Greco, Carlton Colyer and Muneer Ahmad.
Page 26, left to right: Jennifer Aubin, Melissa Shepherd, Pam Sheridan, Carlton Colyer, Muneer Ahmad and Michael Roberts.
Page 34, left to right: Carlton Colyer and Melissa Shepherd.
Page 60, left to right: Cordelia Richards, Tom Dunlop and Chris Smith.
Page 82, left to right: Kevin Dunivan, Carlton Colyer and Dawn Warnocki.
Page 132, Alexis Harman and Chris Bianco.
Page 150, Bambi Soorikian and Henry Schwarz.
Page 155, Peter Reardon and Allison Perley.
Page 174, John Seaglione and Lisa Diaz.
Page 199, Dawn Pisor and Dimitri Rombocos.